TENNESSEE NARRATIVES

TENNESSEE NARRATIVES

TENNESSEE SLAVE NARRATIVES

TENNESSEE SLAVE NARRATIVES

PREPARED FOR PUBLICATION BY
HISTORIC PUBLISHING
All Rights Reserved
San Antonio, Texas
©2017

TENNESSEE NARRATIVES

TENNESSEE SLAVE NARRATIVES

A Folk History of Slavery in the United States From Interviews with Former Slaves

TYPEWRITTEN RECORDS PREPARED BY
THE FEDERAL WRITERS' PROJECT
1936-1938
ASSEMBLED BY
THE LIBRARY OF CONGRESS PROJECT
WORK PROJECTS ADMINISTRATION
FOR THE DISTRICT OF COLUMBIA
SPONSORED BY THE LIBRARY OF CONGRESS

Prepared by
the Federal Writers' Project of
the Works Progress Administration
for the State of Tennessee

WASHINGTON 1941

TENNESSEE NARRATIVES

INFORMANTS

1. INTERVIEW FRANCES BATSON 1213 Scovel St. Nashville, Tennessee
2. INTERVIEW JULIA CASEY 811 9th Avenue, So. Nashville, Tennessee
3. INTERVIEW CECELIA CHAPPEL 705 Allison Street Nashville, Tenn.
4. INTERVIEW WILEY CHILDRESS 808 Gay St. Nashville, Tennessee
5. SUBJECT SLAVE STORIES ROBERT FALLS 608 South Broadway Knoxville, Tennessee Interviewed by Della Yoe, Foreman Federal Writers' Project, First District, WPA Room # 215 Old YMCA Building State and Commerce Streets. Knoxville, Tennessee
6. INTERVIEW RACHEL GAINES 1025 10th Ave. N. Nashville, Tennessee
7. INTERVIEW FRANKIE GOOLE 204 5th Ave. So. Nashville, Tenn.
8. INTERVIEW Precilla Gray 807 Ewing Ave. Nashville, Tenn.
9. INTERVIEW EX-SLAVES JENNY GREER 706 Overton, Street. Nashville, Tennessee
10. INTERVIEW EMMA GRISHAM 1118 Jefferson St. Nashville, Tennessee
11. INTERVIEW MEASY HUDSON 1209 Jefferson St. Nashville, Tennessee
12. INTERVIEW PATSY HYDE 504 9th Avenue N. Nashville, Tennessee
13. INTERVIEW ELLIS KEN KANNON 328 5th Avenue N. St. Mary's Church Nashville, Tennessee
14. INTERVIEW SCOTT MARTIN 438 Fifth Ave., No.
15. INTERVIEW ANN MATTHEWS 719 9th Ave. South Nashville, Tennessee

TENNESSEE NARRATIVES

16. INTERVIEW REV. JOHN MOORE 809 7th Avenue So. Nashville, Tennessee
17. SUBJECT—EX-SLAVE STORIES Andrew Moss #88 Auburn Streets Knoxville, Tennessee
18. SUBJECT—EX-SLAVE STORIES Aunt Mollie Moss # 88- Auburn Street, Knoxville, Tennessee
19. INTERVIEW ANDY ODELL 1313 Pearl Street Nashville, Tennessee
20. INTERVIEW LAURA RAMSEY PARKER 715 Gay St. Nashville, Tennessee
21. INTERVIEW NAISY REECE 710 Overton St. Nashville, Tennessee
22. INTERVIEW MILLIE SIMPKINS "BLACK MAMIE" 1004 10th Avenue, No. Nashville, Tennessee
23. Ex-Slave Stories Subject: Joseph Leonidas Star, # 133 Quebec Place, Knoxville, Tennessee
24. INTERVIEW DAN THOMAS 941 Jefferson Street Nashville, Tennessee
25. INTERVIEW Sylvia Watkins 411 14th Avenue N. Nashville, Tennessee.
26. INTERVIEW NARCISSUS YOUNG Rear 532 1st Street No. Nashville, Tennessee

Transcriber's Notes

TENNESSEE NARRATIVES

[TR: ***] = Transcriber Note
[HW: ***] = Handwritten Note

TENNESSEE NARRATIVES

TENNESSEE NARRATIVES

VOLUME XV

TENNESSEE NARRATIVES

TENNESSEE NARRATIVES

INFORMANTS

Batson, Frances   13

Casey, Julia   15

Chappel, Cecelia   17

Childress, Wiley   20

Falls, Robert   22

Gaines, Rachel   28

Goole, Frankie   30

Gray, Precilla   35

Greer, Jenny   38

Grisham, Emma   39

Hudson, Measy   41

Hyde, Patsy   43

TENNESSEE NARRATIVES

Kannon, Ellis Ken   47

Martin, Scott   50

Matthews, Ann   52

Moore, Rev. John   55

Moss, Andrew   57

Moss, Mollie   62

Odell, Andy   68

Parker, Laura Ramsey   70

Reece, Naisy   72

Simpkins, Millie   73

Star, Joseph Leonidas   77

Thomas, Dan   81

Watkins, Sylvia   83

Young, Narcissus   87

TRANSCRIBER'S NOTES 89

TENNESSEE NARRATIVES

INTERVIEW: FRANCES BATSON
1213 Scovel St.
Nashville, Tennessee

"I dunno jes how ole I ez. I wuz baw'n 'yer in Nashville, durin' slabery. I must be way pas' 90 fer I member de Yankee soldiers well. De chilluns called dem de 'blue mans.' Mah white folks wuz named Crockett. Dr. Crockett wuz our marster but I don't member 'im mahse'f. He d'ed w'en I wuz small. Mah marster wuz mean ter mah mammy w'en her oler chilluns would run 'way. Mah oler br'er went ter war wid mah marster. Mah younger br'er run 'way, dey caught 'im, tuk 'im home en whup'd 'im. He run 'way en wuz nebber found."

"We wuzn't sold but mah mammy went 'way, en lef' me en I got up one mawnin' went ter mah mammy's room, she wuz gon'. I cried en cried fer her. Mah Missis wouldn't let me outa' de house, fer fear I'd try ter find her. Atter freedum mah br'er en a Yankee soldier kum in a waggin en git us. Mah white folks sed, I don' see why you ez takin' dez chilluns. Mah brudder said, 'We ez free now.' I member one whup'in mah missis gib me. Me en her daughter slipped 'way ter de river ter fish. We kotch a fish en mah missis had hit cooked fer us but whup'd us fer goin' ter de river."

"Whar de Buena Vista schul ez hit useter be a Yankee soldiers Barrick. Eber mawnin' dey hadder music. We chilluns would go on de hill, (whar the bag mill ez now) en listen ter dem. I member a black hoss de soldiers had, dat ef you called 'im Jeff Davis he would run you."

"I member de ole well on Cedar Street, neah de Capitol, en six mules fell in hit. Dat wuz back w'en blackberries wuz growin' on de Capitol Hill. En Morgan Park wuz called de pleasure gyarden. En hit wuz full ob Yankee soldiers. Atter de war dere wuz so many

TENNESSEE NARRATIVES

German peeple ober 'yer, dat fum Jefferson Street, ter Clay Street, wuz called Dutch town."

"I wuzn't bawn w'en de sta'rs fell. We didn't git nothin' w'en we wuz freed. Dunno much 'bout de Klu Klux Klan."

"Mah mammy useter tell me how de white folks would hire de slaves out ter mek money fer de marster en she tole me sum ob de marsters would hide dere slaves ter keep de Yankees fum gittin' dem."

"I don' b'leeve in white en black ma'iages. Mah sistah ma'ied a lite man. I wouldin' marry one ef hit would turn me ter gold. Dunno nothin' 'bout votin', allus tho't dat wuz fer de men."

"I can't think ob any tales er nuthin 'bout ghos'. 'Cept one 'bout a marster tyin' a nigger ter a fence en wuz beatin' 'im. A Yankee kum 'long made 'im untie de nigger en den de nigger beat de white man."

"Dis young peeples ez tough. I think half ob dem'll be hung, de way dey throw rocks at ole peoples. Dat's why I's crippled now, a white boy hit me wid a rock. I b'long ter de Methodist Chuch."

"Since freedum I'se hired out, washed en cooked fer diff'ent peeple. De only song I member: 'Hark Fum de Ground dis Mournful Sound.'"

INTERVIEW: JULIA CASEY
811 9th Avenue, So.
Nashville, Tennessee

I wuz bawn in West Tennessee en wuz six y'ars ole w'en war broke out.

Mah Missis wuz Miss Jennie McCullough en she ma'ried Eldridge Casey. Mah Missis's mammy wuz a widder en she gib me, mah mammy, man sistah Violet, mah two br'ers Andrew en Alfred ter Miss Jennie fer a wed'un gif'. Missis Jennie en Marster Eldridge brung us ter Nashville 'fore de war sta'ted.

Mah Missis wuz good ter us. I'se bin w'll tuk keer ob, plenty ter eat en warm clothes ter w'ar. Right now I'se got on long underw'ar en mah chemise.

Mah mammy d'ed fust y'ar ob freedum. Dey tuk her 'way in a two-hoss waggin, 'bout four o'clock one evenin'. Dere wuz no hurses er caskets den. W'en mah mammy d'ed, I still stayed wid Missis Jennie. She raised me. Dat's why folks say I'se so peculiar. De Yankee soldiers tuk mah sistah en two br'ers 'way durin' de war. I ez de mammy ob seven chilluns. All d'ed now but one.

Mah white folks didn't send me ter schul but I'se l'arned a few things ob how ter act. Don't ax me 'bout der young people. Dey ez pas' me. No manners 'tall.

In slavery days you didn't hab ter worry 'bout yo clothes en rations but dese days you hab ter worry 'bout eve'ything.

I 'longs ter de Baptist Chuch. Useter go ter camp-meetin's en hab a big time wid good things ter eat. Didn't go ter de baptizin' much. Dey would leave de chuch singin' en shoutin'. Dere ez three days in

September dat we hab dinnah on de groun' en all Baptist git tergedder. We calls hit de 'sociation.

I'se neber voted cose dat ez de man's job. Mah frens hab nebber had political jobs. Don't b'leeve in ma'rige ob white en black en hit shouldn't be 'lowed.

Since freedom mah main job wuz cookin' but I'se done washin' en ironin'. Atter mah health started failing, I done a lot ob nusin'.

I'se aint abul ter wuk fur de las' five y'ars en de white folks hab he'ped me. De relief gibes me groc'eys, coal en pays mah rent. I hope ter git de ole age pension soon. Mah ole favo'ite song ez "Mazing Grace, How Sweet hit Sounds."

INTERVIEW: CECELIA CHAPPEL
705 Allison Street
Nashville, Tenn.

"I'se bawn in Marshall County, Tennessee. I'm de olest ob ten chilluns en I'se 102 ya'rs ole. I feels lak I'se bin 'yer longer dan dat. Mah mammy wuz brought ter Nashville en sold ter sum peeple dat tuck her ter Mississippi ter live."

"Mah Marster en Missus wuz named Bob en Nancy Lord. Eve'y slave had ter say Missus en Marster en also ter de white babies. I still says hit, en ef I kum ter yo do'r, I nebber kums in 'till you ax me. Lots ob mah folks seze ter me dat I ez too ole fash'on en I seze I don' keer I wuz raised wid manners en too ole ter change."

"Our Marster gib us good food en clothes. I wuz l'arnt how ter nit, weav, sew en spin. On rainy days we wuz gib a certain 'mount ob weavin' ter do en had ter git hit don'. I dunno how ter read er rite. De white folks didn' 'low us ter l'arn nuthin'. I declar' you bettuh not git kotch wid a papah in you han'. Ef I had half a chance lak you chilluns hab, I'd go ter bed wid mah books."

"Our Marster 'lowed us ter go ter chuch. I went bar'foot en had a rag tied 'roun mah haid en mah dress kum up ter mah 'nees. Dat preacher-man would git up dere en tell us "Now you min' yo Marster en Missis en don' steal fum dem." I stayed wid mah Missis fer a long time atter I got freedum en I cried lak a fool w'en I had ter leave dem. Mah Missis seze "You ez jes as free as I ez," but I allus had good clothes en good food en I didn' know how I'd git dem atter I lef' her."

"Mah white folks wuz tight on us but, as ole as I ez, I offun think dat day nebber hit a lick dat I didn' need. Ef'n dey hadn' raised me right, I might hab got in meaness en bin locked up half de time, but

I ain't nebber bin 'rested, en I'se 'ferd ob de policemans. De fiel' slaves wuz whup'd in de fiel's by de oberseer en de Marster en Missis did hit at de house."

"I tell you we had a hahd time. Mah Missis woulden' let dem sell me. I wuz a nuss en house gal. I wuz whup'd wid a bull whup, en got cuts on mah back menny a time. I'se not shamed ter say I got skyars on mah back now fum Marster cuttin' hit wid dat bull whup. Mah Missis also whup'd me. W'en de Missis got ready ter whup me, she would gib us sum wuk ter do, so she would kind ob git ober her mad spell 'fore she whup'd us. Sum times she would lock us up in a dark closet en bring our food ter us. I hated bein' locked up. Atter dey tuk me out ob de house, I wuked in de fiel' lak de urthurs. Long 'fore day break, we wuz standin' in de fiel's leanin' on our hoes waitin' fer daylite en waitin' fer de horn ter blow so we would start ter wuk. Ef'n we wan'ed ter go ter any place we had ter hab a pass wid our Marster's name on hit en ef you didn' hab hit, you got tore ter pieces en den you Marster tore you up w'en you got home."

"One story mah daddy useter tell us wuz 'bout a slave named Pommpy. He wuz allus prayin' fer de good Lawd ter tek 'im 'way. One nite he wuz down on his 'nees prayin', "Good Lawd, kum en tek po Pommpy out ob his misery." De Marster ob Pommpy 'year'd 'm en de Marster made a leetle noise en Pommpy seze, "Who ez dat?" En his Marster seze, "Hits de Lawd kum ter tek po Pommpy out ob his misery." Pommpy crawl under de bed en seze, "Pommpy has bin gon' two er three days."

"'Nurther story: A partridge en a fox 'greed ter kil' a beef. Dey kilt en skinned hit. B'fo dey divide hit de fox said, "Mah wife seze sen' her sum beef fer soup," so he tuck a piece ob hit en carried hit down de hill, den kum back en said mah wife wants mo' beef fer soup. He kep dis up 'til all de beef wuz gon' 'cept de libber. De fox kum back en de partridge seze now lets cook dis libber en both ob us eat hit. De partridge cooked de libber, et hits part rite quick, en den fell ovuh lak hit wuz sick; de fox got skeered en said dat beef ez pizen en he ran down de hill en started bringin' de beef back en w'en he brought hit all back, he lef' en de partridge had all de beef."

"Don't member much now 'bout de Klu Klux Klan en nothin' 'bout slave 'risings at any place. I don' member 'bout de sta'rs fallin', but I did see de comet, en hit looked lak a sta'r wid a long tail; atter freedum, I nebber year'd ob no slave gettin' land er money en I dunno nothin' 'bout de slave mart 'yer fer I didn' git ter kum ter town."

"Since freed, I hab nussed, cooked en don' diff'unt things. I wuk'ed fer one family fifteen y'ars en didn' miss a day. I has stayed at dis place fer de las' five y'ars. I had a stroke en wuz in de hospit'l a long time. I cain' git out; en 'roun' 'yer in de house, I has ter walk wid a stick."

"I ain' nebber voted. One day sum men kum 'yer ter tek me ter vote. I tole dem w'en I got ready ter be a man, I would put on overalls."

"I'se a member ob de Missionary Baptist Chuch. I ain' bin fer a long time kaze I ain' able ter go. De ole song I members ez "Dixie Land," en "Run Nigger Run, de Pat-a rollers Will Git You."

"Oh Lawdy! I think sum ob is young peeple ain' no count w'ile sum ob dem ez alright. I think each color should ma'rie his own color. Hit makes me mad ter think 'bout hit. Ef de good Lawd had wanted dat, he would hab had us all one color."

"Fer a long time de relief gib me a quart ob milk a day, but now all I has ez w'at mah sistah Harriett gibs me. She sin' got much wuk en sum days we don' hab much ter eat. Ef mah Missis wuz livin' I wouldin' go hongry."

INTERVIEW: WILEY CHILDRESS
808 Gay St.
Nashville, Tennessee

"I'se 83 Y'ars ole en wuz bawn a slave. Mah mammy b'longed ter de Bosley's en mah daddy b'longed ter de Scales."

"W'en Miss Jane Boxley ma'ried Marster Jerry Scales, me en mah mammy, br'er en sistah wuz gib ter Miss Jane."

"Durin' de war mah Missis tuk mah mammy en us chilluns wid her ter de mount'ins 'till de war wuz gon'. Did'nt see no soldiers. Don't member now nuthin' 'bout dem Klu Klux men en don't member de ole songs er 'bout slaves votin'."

"Dunno 'bout de young persons, white er black, dey ez all so wild now."

"W'en we all wuz freed we had nuthin en no place ter go, so dat mah mammy lived wid our Missis five y'ars longer."

"De only story dat I member mah people tole me 'bout wuz on Fedd, a slave on de next plantation. He wuz a big man en wuz de strongest man neah dat part ob de kuntry. He wouldin' 'low nobody ter whup 'in. De Marster framed 'im by tellin' 'im ter bring his saddle hoss en w'en he kum wid de hoss several men 'peahrd en tole Fedd dat dey wuz gonna whup 'im. He struck one ob de mans so hahd dey had ter hab de doctuh. De Marster said let 'im 'lone he's too strong ter be whup'd. I'll hab ter shoot 'im. One time Fedd run 'way en de white men whar he stopped know'd he wuz a good fighter en made a $250.00 bet dat nobody could lick 'im. A nigger fum de iron wuks fought Fedd en Fedd won. De iron wuks nigger wuz kilt right dere."

"'fore Freedum de slaves wuz promused forty acres ob land w'en freed but none eber got hit, en I 'year'd ob no one gittin' any money. I dunno nuthin' ob de slave 'risin's, ghostus er dreams, but I member mah folks talkin' 'bout fallin' sta'rs en a comet but I don' member now w'at dey said."

"I'se wuk'd at a lot ob diff'ent jobs since mah freedom. I wuk'd at de Maxwell House 15 years as store room porter, en hit wuz de only wo'th-while hotel in Nashville at dat time. I wuk'd fuh de City fuh menny y'ars en den I wuk'd fuh Foster & Creighton 'till dey wore me out. I off'n think ob deze diff'nt men dat I wuk'd fuh but dey ez all de'd. De las' job I had wuz buildin' fiers en odd jobs fuh a lady up de street. She would gib me food en coal. She ez de'd now."

"I'se not able ter wuk now en all I has ez a small groc'ey order dat de relief gibs me. Dey keep promisin' ter gib me de Old Age Pension en I wish dey would hurry hit up."

TENNESSEE NARRATIVES

SUBJECT: SLAVE STORIES

ROBERT FALLS
608 South Broadway
Knoxville, Tennessee

Interviewed by

Della Yoe, Foreman
Federal Writers' Project,
First District, WPA
Room # 215 Old YMCA Building
State and Commerce Streets.
Knoxville, Tennessee

Robert Falls was born on December 14, 1840, in the rambling one-story shack that accomodated the fifteen slaves of his Old Marster, [HW: Harry] Beattie Goforth, on a farm in Claiborne County, North Carolina. His tall frame is slightly stooped, but he is not subjected to the customary infirmities of the aged, other than poor vision and hearing. Fairly comfortable, he is spending his declining years in contentment, for he is now the first consideration of his daughter, Mrs. Lola Reed, with whom he lives at #608 S. Broadway, Knoxville, Tennessee. His cushioned rocking chair is the honor seat of the household. His apology for not offering it to visitors, is that he is "not so fast on his feet as he used to be."

Despite Uncle Robert's protest that his "mind comes and goes", his memory is keen, and his sense of humor unimpaired. His reminiscences of slave days are enriched by his ability to recreate scenes and incidents in few words, and by his powers of mimicry. "If I had my life to live over," he declares, "I would die fighting rather than be a slave again. I want no man's yoke on my shoulders no more. But in them days, us niggers didn't know no better. All we knowed was work, and hard work. We was learned to say, 'Yes Sir!' and scrape down and bow, and to do just exactly what we was told to do, make no difference if we wanted to or not. Old Marster and Old Mistress would say, 'Do this!' and we don' it. And they say, 'Come here!' and if we didn't come to them, they come to us. And they brought the bunch of switches with them."

"They didn't half feed us either. They fed the animals better. They gives the mules, ruffage and such, to chaw on all night. But they didn't give us nothing to chaw on. Learned us to steal, that's what they done. Why we would take anything we could lay our hands on, when we was hungry. Then they'd whip us for lieing when we say we dont know nothing about it. But it was easier to stand, when the stomach was full."

"Now my father, he was a fighter. He was mean as a bear. He was so bad to fight and so troublesome he was sold four times to my knowing and maybe a heap more times. That's how come my name is Falls, even if some does call me Robert Goforth. Niggers would change to the name of their new marster, every time they was sold. And my father had a lot of names, but kep the one of his marster when he got a good home. That man was Harry Falls. He said he'd been trying to buy father for a long time, because he was the best waggoner in all that country abouts. And the man what sold him to Falls, his name was Collins, he told my father, "You so mean, I got to sell you. You all time complaining about you dont like your white folks. Tell me now who you wants to live with. Just pick your man and I will go see him." Then my father tells Collins, I want you to sell me to Marster Harry Falls. They made the trade. I disremember what the money was, but it was big. Good workers sold for $1,000 and $2,000. After that the white folks didn't have no more trouble with my father. But he'd still fight. That man would fight a she-bear and lick her every time."

"My mother was sold three times before I was born. The last time when Old Goforth sold her, to the slave speculators,—you know every time they needed money they would sell a slave,—and they was taking them, driving them, just like a pack of mules, to the market from North Carolina into South Carolina, she begun to have fits. You see they had sold her away from her baby. And just like I tell you she begun having fits. They got to the jail house where they was to stay that night, and she took on so, Jim Slade and Press Worthy—them was the slave speculators,—couldnt do nothing with her. Next morning one of them took her back to Marse Goforth and told him, "Look here. We cant do nothing with this woman. You got to take her and give us back our money. And do it now,' they says. And they mean it too. So Old Marse Goforth took my mother and give them back their money. After that none of us was ever separated. We all lived, a brother and two sisters and my mother, with the Goforths till freedom."

"And do you know, she never did get over having fits. She had them every change of the moon, or leastways every other moon change. But she kept on working. She was a hard worker. She had to be. Old Mistress see to that. She was meaner than old Marster, she was. She would sit by the spinning wheel and count the turns the slave women made. And they couldn't fool her none neither. My mother worked until ten o'clock almost every night because her part was to 'spend so many cuts' a day, and she couldnt get through no sooner. When I was a little shaver, I used to sit on the floor with the other little fellows while our mothers worked, and sometimes the white folks girls would read us a Bible story. But most of the time we slept. Right there on the floor. Then later, when I was bigger, I had to work with the men at night shelling corn, to take to town early mornings."

"Marster Goforth counted himself a good old Baptist Christian. The one good deed he did, I will never forget, he made us all go to church every Sunday. That was the onliest place off the farm we ever went. Every time a slave went off the place, he had to have a pass, except we didnt, for church. Everybody in thet country knowed that the Goforth niggers didn't have to have no pass to go to church. But that didn't make no difference to the Pattyroolers. They'd hide in the bushes, or wait along side of the road, and when the niggers come from meeting, the Pattyroolers's say, 'Whar's your pass'? Us Goforth niggers used to start running soon as we was out of church. We never got caught. That is why I tell you I cant use my legs like I used to. If you was caught without no pass, the Pattyroolers give you five licks. They was licks! You take a bunch of five to seven Pattyroolers each giving five licks and the blood flows."

"Old Marster was too old to go to the war. He had one son was a soldier, but he never come home again. I never seen a soldier till the war was over and they begin to come back to the farms. We half-grown niggers had to work the farm, because all the famers had to give,—I believe it was a tenth—of their crops to help feed the soldiers. So we didnt know nothing about what was going on, no more than a hog. It was a long time before we knowed we was free. Then one night Old Marster come to our house and he say he wants to see us all before breakfast tomorrow morning and to come on over to his house. He got something to tell us."

"Next morning we went over there. I was the monkey, always acting smart. But I believe they liked me better than all of the others. I just spoke sassy-like and say, "Old Marster, what you got to tell us"? My mother said, "Shut your mouth fool. He'll whip you!" And Old Marster say,—"No I wont whip you. Never no more. Sit down thar all of you and listen to what I got to tell you. I hates to do it but I must. You all aint my niggers no more. You is free. Just as free as I am. Here I have raised you all to work for me, and now you are going to leave me. I am an old man, and I cant get along without you. I dont know what I am going to do." Well sir, it killed him. He was dead in less than ten months."

"Everybody left right now, but me and my brother and another fellow. Old Marster fooled us to believe we was duty-bound to stay with him till we was all twenty-one. But my brother, that boy was stubborn. Soon he say he aint going to stay there. And he left. In about a year, maybe less, he come back and he told me I didnt have to work for Old Goforth, I was free, sure enough free, and I went with him and he got me a job railroading. But the work was too hard for me. I couldnt stand it. So I left there and went to my mother. I had to walk. It was forty-five miles. I made it in a day. She got me work there where she worked."

"I remember so well, how the roads was full of folks walking and walking along when the niggers were freed. Didnt know where they was going. Just going to see about something else somewhere else. Meet a body in the road and they ask, 'Where you going'? 'Dont know.' 'What you going to do'? 'Dont know.' And then sometimes we would meet a white man and he would say, 'How you like to come work on my farm'? And we say, 'I dont know.' And then maybe he say, "If you come work for me on my farm, when the crops is in I give you five bushels of corn, five gallons of molasses, some ham-meat, and all your clothes and vittals whils you works for me." Alright! That's what I do. And then something begins to work up here, (touching his forehead with his fingers) I begins to think and to know things. And I knowed then I could make a living for my own self, and I never had to be a slave no more."

"Now, Old Marster Goforth, had four sisters what owned slaves, and they wasnt mean to them like our Old Marster and Mistress. Some of the old slaves and their folks are still living on their places right to this day. But they never dispute none with their brother about how mean he treat his slaves. And him claiming to be such a Christian! Well, I reckon he's found out something about slave driving by now. The good Lord has to get his work in some time. And he'll take care of them low down Pattyroolers and slave speculators and mean Marsters and Mistress's. He's took good care of me in the years since I was free'd, only now, we needs Him again now and then. I just stand up on my two feet, raise my arms to heaven, and say, 'Lord, help me!' He never fails me. I asked him this morning, didnt I Lola? Asked him to render help. We need it. And here you come. Lola, just watch that lady write. If you and me had her education, we'd be fixed now wouldnt we? I never had no learning."

"Thank you Lady! (tucking the coin into his pocket wallet, along with his tobacco.) And thank you for coming. It does me a heap of good to see visitors and talk about the old times. Come again, wont you? And next time you come, I want to talk to you about old age pensions. I come here from Marian, N.C. three years ago, and they tell me I have to live here four, before I gets a pension. And as I done left North Carolina, I cant get a pension from them. But maybe you can tell me what to do. I likes this place. And I do hopes I get a pension before I gets to be a 'hundred."

INTERVIEW:RACHEL GAINES
1025 10th Ave. N.
Nashville, Tennessee

"Lawdy! I'se dunno how ole I ez. B'leeves I'se 'round 95 ter 100 y'ars. De fust thing I members ez I wuz tuk in a waggin ter Trenton, Kentucky en sold ter Dr. Bainbridge Dickerson jest lak dey sold cows en hosses. Mah sistah wuz sold in de same way at Bowling Green, Kentucky ter 'nuther Marster."

"I wuz sold only one time in mah life en dat wuz w'en Marster Dickinson bought me. Atter freedum wuz 'clared de Marster tole all his slaves dat dey could go wharever'y dey pleased but ef'n dey couldn't mek dere own livin' ter kum ter 'im en he would he'ps dem."

"Missus Dickinson kep' me dere kaze I wuz nuss ter dere son Howard who wuz sho a wild one. I member how he would tote out fried chicken, pig meat en uthuh good stuff ter us darkies. Dey 'greed ter pay me $35.00 a yeah (en keep) en hit wuz gib me eve'y Christmus mawning. Dey treated me good, gib me all de clothes en uthuh things I needed ez ef'n I wuz one ob de fam'ly."

"Eve'y two weeks de Marster would sen' fer Jordan McGowan who wuz de leader ob a string music ban'. Dey would git dere Friday nite early en de slaves would dance in de grape house dat nite en all day Saturday up ter midnite. You don't hab now as good dance music en as much fun as de ole time days had. We allus had a big barbecue er watermelon feast eve'y time we had a dance. Neber 'gin 'll dere be as good times as we useter hab. In mah time we neber y'ard ob wukouses er pen but now dey ez all filled."

"I kin see now in mah mind de ole ice house on de plantation. In de wint'r de slaves would fill hit wid ice dey got off de crik en hit wuz not used 'til warm wedder cum. 'nother thing I members ez de "Pat-a-rollers" (she refers to the Police Patrol of that day) who would kotch en whup runaway slaves en slaves 'way fum dere own plantations widout a pass wid dere Marsters name signed on hit."

"I member w'en Nashville fust had street cars pulled 'long by hosses er mules en I also member de ole dummy cars, run by steam, ter Glendale Park also New Town (now called West Nashville)."

"We had sum bad en good luck signs but I'se fergettin' sum, but I'se members 'bout a black cat crossin' ovuh de path in frunt ob you dat you sho would hab bad luck. W'en dat happened ter me, I would spit on de ground, turn 'round en back ober de place de cat crossed en de "bad luck" wuz gon' fum me. Ef'n you found a ole hoss shoe dat had bin drapt'd by de hoss, hit meant good luck. Sum peeples, white en black, w'en dey fin' a hoss shoe, dey would tack hit up on de frunt door frame wid de toe ter de groun'."

"Atter de Marster en Missus d'ed, I went ter Nashville en made mah way fur menny y'ars by washin' en ironin' fer white peeple but atter I went blind I kum 'yer ter live wid mah daughter."

INTERVIEW: FRANKIE GOOLE
204 5th Ave. So.
Nashville, Tenn.

"I wuz bawn in Smith County on uther side ob Lebanon. Ah'll be 85 y'ars ole Christmas Day.

Mah ole Missis wuz named Sallie, en mah Marster wuz George Waters. Mah mammy's name wuz Lucindia, she wuz sold fum me w'en I wuz six weeks ole, en mah Missis raised me. I allus slept wid her. Mah Missis wuz good ter me, but (her son) mah Marster whup'd me.

Dunno ob any ex-slaves votin' er holdin' office ob any kin.

I member de Ku Klux Klan en Pat-a-rollers. Dey would kum 'roun en whup de niggers wid a bull whup. Ef'n dey met a niggah on de road dey'd say, "Whar ez you gwin dis time ob mawnin'?" De slaves would say, "We ez gwine ovuh 'yer ter stay aw'ile," en den dey would start beatin' dem. I'se stod in our do'er en 'yeard de hahd licks, en screams ob de ones dat wuz bein' whup'd, en I'd tell mah Missis, "Listen ter dat!" She would say, "See, dat ez w'at will happen ter you ef'n you try ter leave." I member one nite a Ku Klux Klan rode up ter our do'er. I tole mah Missis sum body wuz at de do'er wantin' ter know whar mah Marster wuz. She tole 'im he wuz d'ed en her son had gon' 'way dat mawnin'. He hunted all thro de house, en up in de loft, en said whar ez de niggers? Mah Missis tole i'm [TR: 'im] dey wuz down in de lettle house. He went down dere, woke dem up, axed dem 'bout dere Marster en den whup'd all ob dem. Ef de had de Ku Klux Klan now dere wouldn' be so menny peeples on de kounty road en in de pen.

I useter drive up de cows en mah feet would be so cole en mah toes cracked open en bleedin', en I'd be cryin' 'til I got almos' ter de house den I'd wipe mah eyes on de bottom ob mah dress, so de Marster wouldin' know dat I had bin cryin'. He'd say, "Frankie ain't you cryin'?" I'd say, "No suh." "Ez you cole?" "Yes, sir." He would say kum on en warm.

W'en de niggers wuz freed, all ob mah Missis slaves slipped 'way, 'cept me. One mawnin' she tole me ter go down en wake dem up, I went down en knocked, no body said nuthin'. I pushed on de do'er—hit kum op'n—en I fell in de room en hurt mah chin. I went back ter Missis—en she sezs, "W'at ez de matter wid you?" I sezs, "Uncle John en all ob dem ez gon'; I pushed on de do'er en fell in." She sezs you know dey ez not gone, go back en git dem up. I had ter go back, but dey wur'ent dere.

No, I don't member de sta'rs fallin'.

Mah Missis didunt gib me nuthin, cept mah clothes, en she put dem in a carpet bag. Atter freedom mah mammy kum fum Lebanon en got me. Ah'll neber fergit dat day—Oh Lawdy! I kin see her now. Mah ole Missis' daughter-in-law had got a bunch ob switches ter whup me, I wuz standin' in de do'er shakin' all ovuh, en de young Missis wuz tellin' me ter git mah clothes off. I sezs, "I se'd a 'oman kum'g thro de gate." Mah Missis sezs, "Dat ez Lucindia" en de young Missis hid de switches. Mah mammy sezs I'se kum ter git mah chile. Mah Missis tole her ter let me spend de nite wid her, den she'd send me ter de Court House at 9 o'clock next mawnin'. So I stayed wid de Missis dat nite, en she tole me ter alluz be a good girl, en don't let a man er boy trip me. I didunt know w'at she mean but I allus membered w'at she sai. I guess I wuz 'bout 12 y'ars ole w'en I lef' mah Missis en mah mammy brought me ter Nashville en put me ter wuk. De mawnin' I lef' mah Missis, I went ter de Court House en met mah mammy; de Court room wuz jammed wid peeple. De Jedge tole me ter hold my right hand up, I wuz so skeered I stuck both hands up. Jedge sezs,

"Frankie ez dat yo mammy?" I sezs, "I dunno, she sezs she ez." (W'at did I know ob a mammy dat wuz tuk fum me at six weeks ole). He sezs, "Wuz yo Marster good ter you?" I sezs, "Mah Missis wuz, but mah Marster wasn't—he whup'd me." De Jedge said, "Whar did he whup you?" I tole him on mah back. He sezs, "Frankie, ez you laughin'?" I sezs, "No, sir." He said ter mah mammy, "Lucindia tek dis chile en be good ter her fer she has b'en mistreated. Sum day she can mek a livin' fer you." (En thank de Lawd I did keep her in her ole days en wuz able ter bury her.) At dat time money wuz called chin plaster en w'en I lef' out ob de court room diff'ent peeple gib me money en I had mah hat almos' full. Dat was de only money I had gib ter me.

I nussed Miss Sadie Pope Fall; she ma'ried Mat Gardner. I also nussed Miss Sue Porter Houston. I den wuk'd at de Bline Schul.

De fust pa'r ob shoes I eber had wuz atter I kum ter Nashville. Dey had high tops en wuz called bootees. I had sum red striped socks wid dem.

De ole songs I member:

"De Ole Time 'ligion."
 "I'm Goin' ter Join de Ban."

W'en dey would sing deze songs hit would almos' mek you ha'r stand up on yo haid, de way dem peeples would jump en shout!

I member w'en sum ob de slaves run 'way durin' slavery.

I dunno any tales; mah mammy wasn't a 'oman ter talk much. Maybe ef she had bin I would hab had an easier time. As far as I know de ex-slaves hab had diff'ent kinds ob wuk since dere freedum. No, I ain' nebber se'd any ghos'. I'se bin in de woods en dark places, but didn't see nothin', en I'se not goin' ter say I did kaze I might git par'lized.

I went ter schul one y'ar at Fisk in de y'ar 1869.

De last man I wuk'd fer wuz at de Link Hotel. Den I started keepin' boarders. Hab fed all deze Nashville police. De police ez de ones dat hep'ed git deze relief orders fer me. I hab lived on dis street fer 60 years. I lived 22 y'ars whar de Hermitage Laundry ez. Dat ez whar I got de name "Mammie." W'iles livin' dere I raised eighteen chilluns white en black, en sum ob dem iz good ter me now.

I had sum papah's 'bout mah age en diff'ent things, but w'en de back waters got up, dey got lost. I didn't hab ter move but I kep prayin' en talkin' ter de Lawd en I b'leeve he 'Yeard me fer de water didn't git in mah house.

I member w'en de yellow fever en de cholera wuz 'yer, in 1870 en 1873. Dey didn't hab coffins nuff ter put dem in, so dey used boxes en piled de boxes in waggins lak hauling wood.

I'se aint worth a dime now w'en hit kums ter wukin' fer I'se aint able ter do nuthin, thoo I can't complain ob mah livin' since de relief has bin takin' keer ob me.

Dis young peeples, "Oh mah Lawd!" Dey ain' worth talkin' 'bout. I tries ter shame deze 'omen, dey drink (I call hit ole bust haid whiskey), en do such mean things. I'se disgusted at mah own color. Dey try ter know ter much, en dunno muthin', en dey don' do 'nuff wuk.

I nebber voted en dunno nothin' 'bout hit. Hab nebber had any frens in office. Cain' member nothin' 'bout re'structon. I hab bin sick en still don' feel right. Sumtimes I feels krazy.

Hab bin tole dat black cat crossin' road in frunt ob you wuz bad luck. I nebber did b'leeve in any signs. Ef I ez ter hab bad luck, ah'll hab hit.

I b'long ter de Baptist Chuch.

De culored peeples useter hab camp meetin's, en dey'd last fer two weeks. Lawd hab mercy did we hab a time at dem meetin's, preachin', singin', en shoutin'. En ovuh sum whar neah dey would be cookin' mutton en diff'ent good things ter eat. Sum ob dem would shout 'til dere throats would be sore en hit seemed dat sum ob dem niggahs didn't keer ef dey got home ter wuk er not.

I sumtimes wish fer de good ole days. Deze days folks don't hab time fer 'ligion. De dog-gone ole radio en udder things ez takin' hits place.

Oh Lawdie how dey did baptize down at de wha'f! De Baptist peeple would gather at de wha'f on de fust Sunday in May. Dey would kum fum all de Baptist Chuches. Would leave de chuch singin' en shoutin' en keep dat up 'til dey got ter de river. Hab seen dem wid new clothes on git down on de groun en roll en git covered wid dirt. Sum ob dem would almos' luze dere clothes, en dey'd fall down lak dey wuz dying.

Deze last few y'ars dey hab got ter stylish ter shout.

INTERVIEW: Precilla Gray
807 Ewing Ave.
Nashville, Tenn.

I think I'se 107 Y'ars ole. Wuz bawn in Williamson County 'fore de Civil wah. Guess de reason I hab libed so long wuz cose I tuk good keer ob mahself en wore warm clo'es en still do, w'ar mah yarn pettycoats now. Hab had good health all mah life. Hab tuk very little medicine en de wust sickness I eber had wuz small-pox. I'se bin a widah 'bout 70 y'ars.

Mah mammy d'ed w'en I wuz young but mah daddy libed ter be 103 y'ars ole. I nebber went ter schul a day in mah life, ma'ied 'fore freedum en w'en I got free, had ter wuk all de time ter mek a libin' fer mah two chillen. One libes in California en I lives wid de uther, tergedder wid mah great, great, grandson, five y'ars ole, in Nashville.

Mah fust marster en missis wuz Amos en Sophia Holland en he made a will dat we slaves wuz all ter be kep' among de fam'ly en I wuz heired fum one fam'ly ter 'nother. Wuz owned under de "will" by Haddas Holland, Missis Mary Haddock en den Missis Synthia Ma'ied Sam Pointer en I libed wid her 'til freedom wuz 'clared.

Mah fust mistress had three looms en we had ter mek clothes fer ev'ery one on de plan'ashun. I wuz taught ter weav', card, spin en 'nit en ter wuk in de fiel's. I wuz 'feared ob de terbacker wums at fust but Aunt Frankie went 'long by me en showed me how ter pull de wum's head off. Hab housed terbacker till 9 o'clock at nite. Our marster whupped us w'en we needed hit. I got menny a whuppin'.

Marster Amos wuz a great hunter en had lots ob dogs en me en mah cousin had de job ob cookin' dog food en feedin' de dogs. One day de marster went huntin' en lef three dogs in de pen fer us ter feed. One ob de dogs licked out ob de pan en we got a bunch ob switches en started wearin' de dogs out. We thought de marster wuz miles 'way w'en he walked up on us. He finished wearin' de bunch ob switches out on us. Dat wuz a whuppin' I'll nebber fergit.

W'en I wuz heired ter Missis Synthis, I wuked in de fiel's 'til she started ter raise chillens en den I wuz kep in de house ter see atter dem. Missis had a lot ob cradles en dey kep two 'omen in dat room takin' keer ob de babies en lettle chillens 'longin' ter dere slaves. Soon as de chillens, wuz seven y'ars ole, dey started dem ter 'nittin'.

Marster Sam Pointer, husband of Missis Synthis, wus a good man en he wuz good ter us en he fed en clothed us good. We wore yarn hoods, sha'ls, en pantletts which wuz 'nit things dat kum fum yo shoe tops ter 'bove yo knees.

De marster wuz also a 'ligious man en he let us go ter chuch. He willed land fer a culled chuch at Thompson Station. I 'longs ter de foot washin' Baptist, called de Free Will Baptist. De marster bought mah husband William Gray en I ma'ied 'im dere.

W'en de Civil wah wuz startin' dere wuz soldiers an tents eve'ywhar. I had ter 'nit socks en he'ps mek soldiers coats en durin' de wah, de marster sent 100 ob us down in Georgia ter keep de Yankees fum gittin' us en we camped out durin' de whole three y'ars.

I member de Klu Klux. One nite a bunch ob us went out, dey got atter us. We waded a big crik en hid in de bushes ter keep dem fum gittin' us.

Hab gon' ter lots ob camp-meetin's. Dey'd hab lots ob good things ter eat en fed eberbody. Dey'd hab big baptizin's down at de Cumberland Riber and menny things.

W'en freed, our white folks didn't gib us nuthin'. We got 'way en hired out fer an'thin' we could git. Nebber knowed ob any plantashuns [TR: illegible; possibly "men"] be divided. D'ant member 'bout slave 'risings en niggers voting en wuz not ole er'nuff ter member de sta'rs fallin'. Songs we use'ter sing wuz, "On Jordan's Bank I Stand en Cast a Wistful Eye en Lak Drops ob Sweat, Lak Blood Run Down, I Shed mah Tears."

I try not ter think 'bout de ole times. Hit's bin so long ago so I don' member any tales now.

I'se had a lot ob good times in mah day. Our white folks would let us hab "bran dances" an we'd hab a big time. I has nebber voted en I think dat ez a man's wuk. Don't b'leeve in signs, I hab allus tho't whut ez gwine ter be will be, en de only way ter be ez de rite way.

Eber since slavery I'se cooked fer peeple. I cooked fer Mr. Lea Dillon fifteen y'ars. Wuked at de Union Depot fer y'ars. Five y'ars fer Dr. Douglas at his Infirmary en I cooked fer en raised Mrs Grady's baby. Hab wuked fer diff'ent folks ovuh town ter mek mah livin'. I ain't bin able ter wuk fer eight y'ars. Dunno how much I weigh now, I hab lost so much. (she weighs now at least 250 pounds). All de ex-slaves I know hab wuked at diff'ent jobs lak I has.

TENNESSEE NARRATIVES

INTERVIEW
EX-SLAVES
JENNY GREER
706 Overton, Street.
Nashville, Tennessee

"Am 84 y'ars ole en wuz bawn in Florence, Alabama, 'bout seben miles fum town. Wuz bawn on de Collier plantashun en Marster en Missis wuz James en Jeanette Collier. Mah daddy en mammy wuz named Nelson en Jane Collier. I wuz named atter one ob mah Missis' daughters. Our family wuz neber sold er divided."

"I'se bin ma'ied once. Ma'ied Neeley Greer. Thank de Lawd I aint got no chilluns. Chilluns ez so bad now I can't stand dem ter save mah life."

"Useter go ter de bap'isin's en dey would start shoutin' en singin' w'en we lef' de chuch. Went ter deze bap'isin's in Alabama, Memphis, en 'yer in Nashville. Lawdy hab mercy, how we useter sing. Only song I members ez 'De Ole Time 'ligion.' I useter go ter camp meetin's. Eve'rbody had a jolly time, preachin', shoutin' en eatin' good things."

"We didn't git a thing w'en we wuz freed. W'en dey said we wuz free mah people had ter look out fer demselves."

"Don' member now 'bout K.K.K. er 'structshun days. Mah mammy useter tell us a lot ob stories but I'se fergot dem. I'se neber voted en dunno ob any frens bein' in office."

"No mam, no mam, don't b'leeve in diff'ent colurs ma'rin. I member one ole sign—'bad luck ter empty ashes atter dark.'"

"I'se hired out wuk'n in white folks house since freedum. I'se a widow now en live 'yer wid mah neice en mah sistah."

INTERVIEW: EMMA GRISHAM
1118 Jefferson St.
Nashville, Tennessee

"I wuz bawn in Nashville. I'se up in 90 y'ars, but I tell dem I'se still young. I lived on Gallatin Pike long 'fore de war, an uster se'd de soldiers ride by."

"Mah marsters name wuz Wm. Penn Harding. Mah daddy wuz sold at Sparta, Tennessee 'fore I wuz bawn en Marster Harding bought 'im. Mah mammy erready 'longed ter de Hardings."

"I don' member much 'bout slavery I wuz small, but I know I wore a leetle ole slip wid two er three bottons in frunt. Mammy would wash me en I'd go out frunt en play wid de white chilluns."

"W'en de fightin' got so heavy mah white peeple got sum Irish peeple ter live on de plantation, en dey went south, leavin' us wid de Irish peeple."

"I wuz leetle en I guess I didn't think much 'bout freedum, I'd allus had plenty ter eat en w'ar."

"Dunno ob any slaves gittin' nuthin at freedum."

"Our white folks didn't whup mah peeple; but de oberseers whup'd de slaves on uther plantations."

"De Yankees had camps on de Capitol hill. En dere wuz soldier camps in east Nashville en you had ter hab a pass ter git thro?"

"I member w'en de pen wuz on 15th en Chuch, en de convicts wuk'd 'round de Capitol."

"I went ter schul at Fisk a short time, w'en hit wuz neah 12th en Cedar, en a w'ile down on Chuch St. Mah teacher allus bragged on me fer bein' clean en neat. I didn't git much schuling, mah daddy wuz lak mos' ole folks, he though ef'n you knowd yo a, b, c's en could read a line, dat wuz 'nuff. En he hired me out. Dunno w'at dey paid me, fer hit wuz paid ter mah daddy."

"I wuz hired ter a Mrs. Ryne fer y'ars, whar de Loveman store ez now. Dere wuz a theatre whar Montgomery Ward store ez, a lot ob de theatre peeple roomed en bo'ded wid Mrs. Ryne, en dey would gib me passes ter de sho' en I'd slip up in de gall'ry en watch de sho'. I couldn't read a wud but I 'joy'd goin'. Mah daddy wuz a driver fer Mr. Ryan."

"I nussed fer a Mrs. Mitchell en she had a boy in schul. One summer she went 'way. A Mrs. Smith wid 10 boys wanted me ter stay wid her 'til Mrs. Mitchell got back en I staid en laked dem so well dat I wouldin go back ter Mrs. Mitchell's."

"I went ter Memphis en ma'ied George Grisham in 1870. He jinned de army, as ban' leader, went ter San Antonio, Texas en I kum back ter Mrs. Smith's en stayed 'til her mammy lost her mind. Mah husband d'ed in Texas, fum heart truble. All his things wuz sent back ter me, en eve'y month I got a $30.00 pension fer me en mah daughter. W'en she wuz 16 dey cut hit down en I only git $12.00 now."

"I edj'cated mah daughter at Fisk; en she's bin teachin' schul since 1893. She buy dis place en we live tergedder. We hab good health en both ez happy. I hab a 'oman kum eve'y Monday en wash fer us."

"De ole songs I member ez:

"Harp fum de Tomb dis Mournful Sound."
"Am I a soldier ob de Cross."

"Ole signs ez: Dream ob snakes, sign ob de'th.—Ef a hen crows a sign ob de'th.—Sneeze wid food in mouth means de'th.—Ef a black cat crosses de road, walk backwards 'til you git pas' whar hit crossed. Mah parents useter tell lots ob tales but I can't think ob dem."

"Oh honey, I dunno w'at dis young peeples ez kum'n ter. Dey ez so diff'ent fum de way I wuz raised. I don't think much ob dis white en black mar'ages. Hit shouldn't be 'lowed."

"I 'long ter de Missionary Baptist."

INTERVIEW: MEASY HUDSON
1209 Jefferson St.
Nashville, Tennessee

"Wuz bawn' in North Carolina en I'se 90 y'ars ole in November. W'en war broke out we kum ter Tennessee en hab bin 'yer eber since. Wuz 'yer w'en old Hood fi'rd de cannons. He said he wuz kum'n 'yer ter Christmas dinnah, but he didn't do hit."

"Mah white folks wuz named Harshaw. Marster Aaron Harshaw d'ed en we wuz willed ter his chilluns en dat we wuz not ter be whup'd er 'bused in anyway. We wuz sold, but long 'fore de war mah daddy wuz freed en mah manny wuz not freed, but kep' a slave."

"De marster's chilluns wuz small en eber New Y'ar Day, we wuz put on a block en hired out ter de high bidduh, en de money spent ter school de marster's chilluns."

"I wuz tole dat sum ob de white peeples wuz so mean ter dere slaves dat de slaves would tek a pot en turn hit down in a hollow ter keep dere whites fum yearin' dem singin' en prayin'. De Ku Klux wuz bad on de ex-slaves at fust."

"De white folks 'fore de war had w'at dey called "Muster" en I would go down wid dem. I would dance en de folks would gib me money er gib me candy en durin' de war de soldiers wuz de prettiest things."

"Got nuthin' at freedum en wuz not lookin' fuh nuthin'. Ef marster had lived he might hab gib us sump'in. He wuz a good man en good ter us. Eber since mah freedum, I'se wuk'd as a laundress. Wuk'd fer one fam'ly ober 21 y'ars. 'Bout two y'ars ago I lefted a tub, en hurt mahself. I'se not able ter wuk now. I hab bin ma'ied twice en I'se voted three times."

"I went ter schul at Fisk, a short time, w'en hit wuz on 12th Avenue, but I diden' git ter go long 'nuff ter git en edj'cation."

"Jis 'fore de Civil War I members de comet. Hit wuz lak a big sta'r wid a long tail. Eve'body said hit wuz a sign ob Judgement Day."

"Bad luck signs: Ef'n a picture falls, hit's a sign ob de'th—bad luck ter step ovuh a broom—ef a clock stop runnin' en later hit strike, dat means de'th."

"Sum ob de young peeple terday ez good but sum ob dem don't wan'ter be nuthin'. De last war ruined mos' ob de white en de black."

"I b'leeves in de Baptist 'ligion en 'longs ter de Baptist Church, 9th Avenue N. on Cedar Street. De white 'oman I wuk'd fuh wan'ed me ter join de Christian (colored) chuch. Only song I now members ez "On Jordans Banks I Stand." "Don't think dis marrin' ob whites wid blacks should be 'lowed en think eve'y culor should stay ter hitssef."

"I don't member now 'bout any stories tole back in ole times. Our white folks wuz Christians en tried ter teach us right en dey diden' tek up much time tellin' stories."

INTERVIEW: PATSY HYDE
504 9th Avenue N.
Nashville, Tennessee

"Dunno how ole I ez. I wuz bawn in slavery en b'longs ter de Brown family. Mah Missis wuz Missis Jean R. Brown en she wuz kin ter Abraham Lincoln en I useter y'ar dem talkin' 'bout 'im livin' in a log cabin en w'en he d'ed she had her house draped in black. Marster Brown wuz also good ter his slaves. De Missis promus Marster Brown on his de'th bed nebber ter let us be whup'd en she kep her wud. Sum ob de oberseers on urthur plantations would tie de slaves ter a stake en gib dem a good whup'in fer sump'in dey ought not ter done."

"All cul'ed people wore cotton goods en de younger boys run 'round in der shurt tails. Mah Missis nit all de white chilluns stockin' en she made me sum. I had ter hold de yarn on mah hans w'en she wuz nittin'. I members one time I wuz keepin' flies off de table usin' a bunch ob peacock feathers en I went ter sleep standin' up en she tole me ter go back ter de kitchen." "I went en finish mah nap."

"One day ole Uncle Elick woke Marster Brown fum his atter-noon nap tellin' 'im dat de prettiest men dat I ever seed wuz passin' by on de road. He went ter de winder en said, "Good Gawd, hit's dem damn Yankees." Mah white folks had a pretty yard en gyarden. Soldiers kum en camped dere. I'd slip ter de winder en lissen ter dem." "W'en dey wuz fightin' at Fort Negley de cannons would jar our house. De soldier's ban' play on Capitol Hill, en play "Rally 'roun' de Flag Boys, Rally 'roun de Flag."

"De slaves would tek dere ole iron cookin' pots en turn dem upside down on de groun' neah dere cabins ter keep dere white folks fum hearin' w'at dey wuz sayin'. "Dey claimed dat hit showed dat Gawd wuz wid dem."

"In slavery time peeples b'leeved in dreams. I members one nite I dreamed dat a big white thing wuz on de gatepost wida haid. I tole mah mammy en she said, "Gawd wuz warning us." De ma'rige cer'mony in de days ob slavery wuz by de man en 'oman jumpin' ovuh a broom handle tergedder."

"I don' member much 'boud de Ku Klux Klan, but I does member seein' dem parade one time in Nashville." (She evidently refers to the Klan's last parade in 1869 in Nashville, immediately preceeding the disbandment of the Klan at Fort Negley.)

"I members dat de northern soldier's ban' would play Union Ferever, Rally 'roun de Flag, en Down Wid de Traitors en up Wid de Sta's en Stripes."

"De songs I members ez:

I'se a Soldier ob de Cross.
 Follow de Lamb.
 I would not Live Allus.
 I Axs not ter Stay."

"I member w'en de stars fell. Hit wuz so dark en eberbody wuz skeered, en I member a comet dat looked lak a big red ball en had sump'in lak a tail on hit. Eber one wuz skeered en wuz 'feard hit would hit de groun' en burn de worl' up. I member de fust street lites in Nashville. W'en de lamp mans would kum 'round en lite de lamps dey would yell out "all ez well" en I also members de Southern money goin' out en Yankee money kum'n in, en also w'en dere wuzn't any coal 'yer en eve'ythin' wuz wood en mos' ob dis town wuz in de woods."

"De slaves wuz tole dey would git forty ak'rs ob groun' en a mule w'en dey wuz freed but dey nebber got hit. W'en we wuz free we wuz tuned out widout a thing. Mah grandmammy wuz an "Ole mammie" en de Missis kep her. Atter freedum a lot ob Yankee niggah gals kum down 'yer en hire out."

"W'en I wuz a young girl hund'eds ob people went ter de wharf at de foot ob Broadway on de fust Sunday in May ob eber'y year fer de annual baptizin' ob new members inter de Baptist (culored) churches ob de city. Thousands ob white people would crowd both sides ob de Cumberland Riber, Broadway en de Sparkman Street Bridge ter witnus de doin's. On leavin' de chuches de pastor would lead de parade ter de wharf. Dey would sing en chant all de way fum de chuch ter de river en sum ob de members would be ovuhkum wid 'ligious feelin' en dey would hop up en down, singin' en shoutin' all de time, or may be dey would start ter runnin' down de street en de brethern would hab ter run dem down en bring dem back."

"We useter hav' dem champ meetin's en dey wuz "honeys," en I enjoy dem too. We wore bandanna handkerchiefs on our haids en long shawls ovuh our shoulders. At deze meetin's dey had all kinds ob good things ter eat en drink."

"Atter mah freedum I dun washin' en Ironin' fer white families. Neber ma'ried but I neber worries no matter w'at happens en dat's may be cause ob mah livin' so long."

"Things ter day ez mighty bad. Not lak de ole days. Worl' ez gwin ter end soon."

"Atter I got ter feeble ter do washin' en ironin' fer mah livin', I went ter de Relief Office ter git dem ter he'ps me, but dey wouldn't do a thing. I had no place ter go er no money ter do wid. Dis culid 'oman tuk me in en does all she can fer me but now she ez disable ter wuk en I dunno w'at ter do. Ef'n I could git a small grocer order each week til I git de ole Age Pension hit would he'p lots."

INTERVIEW: ELLIS KEN KANNON
328 5th Avenue N.
St. Mary's Church
Nashville, Tennessee

"I dunno jes how ole I ez. I wuz bawn in Tennessee as a slave. Mah mammy kum frum Virginia. Our marster wuz Ken Kannon."

"Our Mistress wouldn't let us slaves be whup'd but I member mah daddy tellin' 'bout de Overseer whuppin' 'im en he run 'way en hid in a log. He tho't de blood hounds, he heered 'bout a half mile 'way, on his trail could heer 'im breathe but de hounds nebber fin' 'im. Atter de hounds pas' on, mah daddy lef' de log hidin' place en w'en he got ter a blacksmith shop, he se'ed a white man wid a nigger who had handcuffs on en w'en de white man tuk off de handcuffs, de nigger axed mah daddy whar he wuz gwine en he tole 'im back ter mah Mistress en de nigger sezs I ez too. Mah daddy slipped 'way fum 'im en went home."

"W'en I wuz a young boy, I didn't wear nothin' but a shirt lak all urthur boys en hit wuz a long thing lak a slip dat kum ter our knees. Our Mistress had a big fier place en w'en we would kum in cole she would say ain't you all cole. (You all was always used in the plural and not singular as some writers have it). W'ile we wuz warmin' she often played de organ fer us ter heer."

"I waited on mah Marster 'til he d'ed. Dey let me stay rite wid de body. Mah Mistress, Mammy ob de Marster, wuz in bad health at dat time, en 'fore we sta'ted ter de graveyard, I put a feather bed in de car'age en got a pitcher ob water ready en 'fore we git dere she got awful sick."

"Durin' slavery de slaves hadder keep quiet en dey would turn a kittle upside down ter keep de white folks 'yearin dere prayers en chants. W'en a slave wanted ter go ter 'nother plantation he had ter hab a pass. Ef' dey disobeyed dey got a whuppin, en ef dey had a pass widout de Marsters signature dey got a whuppin. Ef'n dey had ter hab passes now dere wouldin' be no meaness."

"I member de Klu Klux Klan kumin ter mah daddy's home axin fer water en dey would keep us totin' water ter dem fer fifteen ter twenty minutes. Dey didn't whup er hurt any ob us. I also member 'yearin mah mammy en daddy tellin' us 'bout de sta'rs fallin'. I member de comet. Hit wuz a big ball en had a long tail."

"I hab 'yerd dem tell 'bout Mr. Robertson. He wuz mean ter his slaves en dey sezs dey could see a ball ob fier rollin' on de fence en w'en dey would git ter de spring, a big white thing lak a dog would crawl under de rock. De slaves wuz natur'ally superstitious en b'leeved in dreams, ole sayings en signs. I hab mahse'f se'ed things dat I ain't onderstan'. Hab almost seen de things dat (apostle) John seed."

"Dunno nuthin 'bout any ob de ex-slaves voting er de Nat Turner 'Bellion."

"Atter freedum mos' ob de slaves wuk'd fer dere livin' jes as I ez. De men in de fiel's, de 'omen in de house. I wuk'd at a hotel in McMinnville en one day, I wuz keepin' de flies off de table wid a brush made frum fine strips ob papah en de string broke en hit fell on de table. One man jumped up grabbed a cheer sayin' ah'll knock you down wid dis cheer."

"De slave 'pected ter git 40 akers ob land en a mule but nobody eber got hit as fur as I know. We didn't git nuthin. Our white peeple wuzzent able ter gib us anyting. Eve'ythin' dey had wuz tuk durin' de wah. Dey wuz good ter us an stuck wid us en mah peeple stayed wid mah Mistress."

"Dis young gineratshun ob niggers, I 'clare dey ez jes 'bout gon'. Dey won't wuk, all's stealin' en mabe wuk long 'nuff ter git a few clothes ter strut 'round in. I may be wrong but dat ez mah hones' pinion."

"De songs—I member ez:

De Ole Ship ob Zion.
Do You Think You'll be Able ter tek me Home."

"I has bin 'yer fifteen y'ars en hab wuked onder two Priests en now wukin under de third. Dey hab all bin nice ter me. Hab neber had any trubble wid white peeple en you'd be sprized how good dey ez ter me. Dey don't treat me lak a nigger."

"Eber since I got mah freedum en 'fore I got dis chuch job, I dun all kinds ob odd jobs, waited on tables, pressin' clothes en anyting else dat kum 'long, but sum jobs wuz small pay but hit kep me 'live."

"Don't member any slave uprisin's. Our peeple wuz good ter us."

INTERVIEW: SCOTT MARTIN
438 Fifth Ave., No.

"I'se 90 y'ars ole and wuz bawn in slavery in Sumner County, Tennessee and I b'long to Marster Dr. Madison Martin an' mah Misses Mary. And I wuk'd wid de stock an' wuz de houseman."

"I hab neber been in any truble, neber 'rested en neber bin in jail. I knows how ter behave, but de young peeples ob terday ain' dun rite en dey don' 'mounts ter much. Dar am a few dat am all rite. In de ole days dey wer' bettuh dan dey ez terday. De white and black ougher not ma'rie."

"I has voted two times, but I disremembers who I voted fer. Neber hadney frens in office en I nebr met any of de Klu Klux men. I didn' go out much en I neber wuz kotched w'en I did git out. I heered lots 'bout nigger uprisin' but dey wuz away off."

"I b'long ter de Missionary Baptist chuch an' I useter preach in mah chuch 'ouse en udders w'en called. Once a y'ar I wud be at de Cumberland Riber wha'f en' baptiz' culled peeples all da'. We useter hab camp meetin' in de ole days en hab good things ter eat en I would preach all day. I went ter schul two sessions en den I went to wuk."

"I member de fust street kar line that run on East side of Cumberland Riber ter East end ob de ole wood bridge dat de 'arly settlers build. De kars wer' pulled by hosses en' mules. De whites en blacks mixed tergedder en den de law made de whites rid' in frunt en the blacks in de rearuh. I think dat wuz rite, but sum ob mah race wuz mad 'bout hit. I wuz on a kar one day and mules run'd 'way en de ole red mule got loose frum de kar en run'd ober a mile 'fore dey ketched him en dey brot 'im ba'k en de kar' pas' on. I members de ole L & N Railroad on de East side. W'en my folks wud ride de train dey had 'ter hold me tite or I wuld git 'way frum dem en run en hide 'hind sum logs. I wuz scar'et ter ride on de kars."

"Atter freedum de slaves had'n no truble ter go whar dey wan'. Menny lef' but menny stay wid der ole marsters. I stay wid my marster tell he d'ed. I den kum an' lib wid mah daddy on Lebanon Road. Atter dat I libed on Gallatin Road an' den I kum ter Nashville, an' wuk wid pic' and shovel on streets, sewers an' udder jobs. I heered dem sez dat de slaves wud git lan', hoss, money er sumpin' but I neber heerd ob nobody gittin nuthin'. Dere wuz not slave 'raisings eroun' whar I wuz."

"De fallin' st'ars wuz 'fore mah time, but I'se heer'd mah daddy tole 'bout hit. I se'd de comet wid hit shinnin' tail an' I fust b'leevd sumbody put hit up dere."

"Good luck sign wuz w'en a stray cat kum ter yo' house an' stay dere. Bad luck sign wuz a black kat crossin' yo' path in frunt ob yer. Ter ke'p frum havin' de bad luck yo' back up pas' whar hit crossed yer path en den spit an' yer hab no bad luck."

"Dem air ships luk nice but dey ez spoke 'boud in de Holy Bible, dat sum day dere wud be flyin' things in de air'h an' I think dat dese things am it. De otomobeels kiver nuder passag' in de Bible which seze de peeple 'll rid' on de streets widout hosses en mules."

"Mah fav'rite songs am "I Gwine to Jine de Gideon Band," and "Keep Yo' Lits Bunnin'.""

"Ter ole now ter wuk an' mah haid don' se'm ter be tergedder an' I'se gits he'ps frum de Welfare."

TENNESSEE NARRATIVES

INTERVIEW: ANN MATTHEWS
719 9th Ave. South
Nashville, Tennessee

"I wuz bawn in Murfreesboro on Stones River. I dunno how ole I ez en hit meks me 'shamed ter tell peeple dat, but mah mammy would hit me in de mouth w'en I'd ax how ole I wuz. She say I wuz jes' tryin' ter be grown."

"Mah mammy's name wuz Frankie en mah daddy wuz Henry Ken Kannon. Don' member much 'bout mah mammy 'cept she wuz a sho't fat Indian 'oman wid a turrible tempah. She d'ed, durin' de war, wid black measles."

"Mah daddy wuz part Indian en couldn't talk plain. W'en he go ter de store he'd hab ter put his han' on w'at he want ter buy. He d'ed eight months 'fore de Centennial."

"Our marster en missis wuz Landon en Sweenie Ken Kannon. Dey wuz good ter us, en we had'n good things ter eat."

"I member de Yankee en Southern soldiers. One day me en mah young missis, en sum chilluns went up ter de road en we se'ed sum Yankee soldiers kumin', I clum'ed on de fence, de urthurs run 'way en hid. One ob de soldiers sezs ter me, 'Lettle girl who wuz dat wid you,' en I sezs, 'Hit wuz Miss Puss en sum chilluns.' He laughed en sezs, 'You ez brave ain' you?'"

"Our missis let us go ter chuch. I 'long ter de chuch ob Christ."

"I dunno ob but one slave dat got lan' er nothin' w'en freedum wuz 'clared. We didn't git nuthin at freedum. Mah daddy went back in de woods en built us a saplin house en dobbed hit wid mud. Atter freedum mah daddy went 'way, en we chilluns staid in dat house in de woods by oursel's. Dere wuz two weeks we didn't see a bit ob bre'd. I went up w'at ez called de nine mile cut neah Tullahoma, en axed a 'oman ef she would let us hab sum bre'd. She gib me sum meat en bre'd, en tole me ter kum back. I went back home en we et sump'in, en I went back ter de 'oman's house, she gib me a sack ob flour en a big piece ob midlin' meat. We wuz skeered, bein' dere 'lone so I would set up wile mah br'ers slep', den I'd sleep in de daytime. One nite sumbody knocked at de do'er en hit wuz mah daddy en he had two sacks ob food, en de urthur chilluns got up en we et a big meal."

"I useter 'yer de folks talk 'bout de sta'rs fallin', but dat happen' 'fore I wuz bawn."

"I didn't go ter schul, mah daddy wouldin' let me. Said he needed me in de fiel wors den I needed schul. I wuz allus sassy en stubbun. I run 'way fum mah daddy en kum ter Nashville. I stayed at a schul on Franklin Pike, run by Mrs. McGathey. I wuz de only cul'ed person dere. Dey wuz good ter me en eve'y Chrismus I would git a big box ob clothes en things."

"In Manchester de Klu Klux Klan wore big high hats, red handkerchiefs on dere faces en red covers on dere hosses. Dey tuk two niggers out ob jail en hung dem ter a chestnut tree."

"One nite w'en I wuz gwine wid mah daddy fum de fiel' home, we met sum ob de K.K.K. en dey said, 'Ain't you out late Henry? En who ez dat gal wid you?' Mah daddy said, 'We ez gwine home fum wuk, en dis ez mah daughter.' Dey said, 'Whar has she bin, we ain't nebber se'ed her.' He told dem, 'I'd bin in Nashville.' Dey said dey'd be back dat nite but we didn't see dem."

"W'en I wuz in Manchester I promus de Lawd I wouldin' dance. But one nite I wuz on de ball floor, dancin' fum one end ob de room ter de urthur en sump'in sezs go ter de do'er. I didn't go right den en 'gin hit sezs you ez not keepin' yo promus. I went ter de do'er en you could pick a pin off de groun' hit wuz so light. In de sky wuz de prettiest thing you ebber se'ed, so many culors, blue, white, green, red en yellow."

"Since freedum I'se wuked wid diff'ent peeple, cookin' en keepin' house. I'se de mammy ob three chilluns. Two ob dem ez 'way fum 'yer, en I live 'yer wid mah daughter."

"Old songs, I member ez:

Dark wuz de Nite.
 I'll Live wid Gawd Forever, Bye en Bye.
 Fum dis Earth I go, Oh Lawd, W'at Will 'kum ob Me."

"So yer wan't me ter tell you de truf? I think de young peeple ez nothin'. Dey think dey ez smaht. Most ob de ex-slaves I'se knowed has cooked en nussed, done laundry wuk; wuked in fiel's en diff'ent things."

"I'se neber voted en hab neber paid any 'tention ter de niggers gittin' ter vote. Don't hab any frens in political office. Can't member any tales er signs."

"I don't b'leeve in dese mixed white and black families en hit shouldn't be 'lowed."

"Durin' slavery de white folks didn't want de niggahs ter sing en pray, but dey would turn a pot down en meet at de pot in de nite en sing en pray en de white folks wouldn't 'yer dem."

"Ef a slave died de white folks wouldn't let nobody set up wid de body 'cept de niggers ob dat plantation, but urthur slaves would slip in atter dark, set up en den slip back ter dere plantation 'fore day."

"W'en I useter go ter camp meetin' dey had big dinnahs en spread hit on de groun'. Dey preached, sung, shouted en eve'ybody had a good time."

"Fum de camp meetin's dey would go ter de wharf en baptize. Dey would tie handkerchiefs 'roun dere haids. W'en dey wuz dipped under de water sum ob dem would kum up shoutin'."

A TALE

One time de preacher wuz in de river fixin' ter baptize a man. Eve'ybody wuz singin' ole time 'ligion. A 'oman sung, "I don' lak dat thing 'hind you." Bout dat time de pahson en de udder man se'd an alligator. De parson sezs, "No-By-God I Don't Either." He turned de man loose en dey both run 'way.

INTERVIEW: REV. JOHN MOORE
809 7th Avenue So.
Nashville, Tennessee

"I wuz bawn in Georgia (exact time not known) en mah mammy wuz half Indian en mah daddy a slave. Both ob dem owned by William Moore. Sum time atter dat Marster Moore sold mah daddy en den de Moore Sistuhs looked atter me en wuz allus good ter me. "Lawdy, dey wuz good white folks."

"Durin' slavery times de slaves would hab ter git fum dere marster a pas' 'fore dey could visit dere own people on de uther plantations. Ef'n you had no pass you would git in trouble ef caught wid out one which allus ment a good whuppin' w'en dey returned. At dat time menny slaves would run 'way en hide in caves en menny ob dem would go by de "ondergroun' railroad" ter Canada whar slavery wuz not recognized." (The underground railroad consisted of hiding places throughout the states to Canada and the slaves would make the trip under cover from station to station.)

"De slaves would slip out at nite ter private meetin's en turn a pot bottom up on de groun' en leave a little hole under hit so de sound ob dere talkin' would go onder de pot en no one would 'year whut dey wuz talkin' 'bout."

"De ex-slaves ob de better class did vote en de white peeple stuck wid de good cul'ed folks. I don' member now 'bout de Nat Turner 'Bellion."

"Atter freedum de slaves wuz 'lowed ter stay on de plantation en 'lowed ter farm en gib half dey made. Atter slavery I useter wuk fer fifty cents en git a peck ob meal, three pounds ob bacon en a quart ob syrup which would las' a week."

"De Ku Klux Klan's plan wuz ter whup all white er cul'ed people dat didn't stay at home en support dere families but would run 'roun en live a bad life. W'en de Klan would be passin' through de slaves would call dem ghostus."

"One nite mah br'er en me wuz sleepin' in de dining room. Sumpin woke us an we seed sumpin' dat kum through de yard en got hold ob sum blocks. Dat thing didn't hab no haid en didn't hab no tale en looked lak hit wuz backin' up on all four legs. Nex mawnin' we could fin' no tracks ob whuteber hit wuz en de gate wuz also fasened."

"Dis young peoples 'cordin' ter de Bible ez on de broad road ter ruin. Dey think dey ez as good as de white people but dey ez classed as niggahs in mah eyes."

"Caint member any ob de ole songs now."

SUBJECT—EX-SLAVE STORIES

ANDREW MOSS
#88 Auburn Streets
Knoxville, Tennessee

"One ting dat's all wrong wid dis world today," according to Andrew Moss, aged negro, as he sits through the winter days before an open grate fire in his cabin, with his long, lean fingers clasped over his crossed knees, "is dat dey ain no 'prayer grounds'. Down in Georgia whar I was born,—dat was 'way back in 1852,— us colored folks had prayer grounds. My Mammy's was a ole twisted thick-rooted muscadine bush. She'd go in dar and pray for deliverance of de slaves. Some colored folks cleaned out knee-spots in de cane breaks. Cane you know, grows high and thick, and colored folks could hide de'seves in dar, an nobody could see an pester em."

"You see it was jes like dis. Durin' de war, an befo de war too, white folks make a heap o fun of de colored folks for alltime prayin. Sometime, say, you was a slave en you git down to pray in de field or by de side of de road. White Marster come 'long and see a slave on his knees. He say, 'What you prayin' 'bout?' An you say, 'Oh, Marster I'se jes prayin' to Jesus cause I wants to go to Heaven when I dies.' An Marster say, 'Youse my negro. I git ye to Heaven. Git up off'n your knees.' De white folks what owned slaves thought that when dey go to Heaven de collored folk's would be dar to wait on em. An ef'n it was a Yank come 'long, he say too, 'What you prayin' 'bout?' You gives de same 'sponse. An he say, 'We'se gwine save you. We goin' to set you free. You wants to be free, dont you?' 'Yessir, Boss!' 'Well den, Yank say, come go 'long wid me.' Ain no use keep sayin' 'Please sir Boss, I'll have to arsk my

Master.' Yank say, 'what you mean, Marster? You aint got no Marster. We's settin' you free.'"

"Sometimes dey takes a' tie a rope 'round you, and they starts ridin' off but dey dont go too fas' so you walks behind. Sometimes 'long comes another Yank on a horse an he arsk, 'Boy ain you tired?' 'Yessir Boss.' 'Well den you git up here behind me and ride some.' Den he wrop de rope all 'round de saddle horn. Wrops and wrops, but leaves some slack. But he keeps you tied, so's you wont jump down and run away. An many's de time a prayin' negro got took off like dat, and want never seen no more."

"'Course ef'n you goes wid em, you 'member your trainin' and 'fore you leaves de field, you stacks your hoe nice, like you was quittin' de days work. Dey learned the little'uns to do dat, soon's dey begins to work in de fields. Dey had little hoes, handles 'bout de size of my arm, for de little fellers. I've walked many a mile, when I was a little feller, up and down de rows, followin' de grown folks, an chopping wid de hoe 'round de corners whar de earth was soft so de little uns could hoe easy. Whoopee! Let dat dinner horn blow, and evy body stacks dey hoes, nince, neat stacks standin up, and starts to run. Some eats in dey own cabins, but dem what eats at de big house, sets down at a long table, and gets good grub too! Evy night, our Marster give us evy one a glass o whiskey. Dat's to keep off decease. Mornins' we had to all drink tar water for de same purpose. Dat want so tasty."

"My Marster's name was George Hopper. Dat man paid taxes on more'n two-thousand acres of land in two counties. I lived in dem two counties. Was born in Wilkes and raised in Lincoln County, Georgia. We called it de middle-south. My Marster he never did marry. Lots of folks didnt, dey jes took up wid one another. Marster Hopper had five children by my grandmother. She was his house woman, dat's what he call 'er. An when he died he willed her and all dem chilluns a house, some land, and a little money. He'd of left em a heap more money and ud been one of the richest men in the country, ef'n de war hadn't broke out. When it was over he had a barrel full of 'Federate greenbacks. But t'want no count. He done broke den. One day my uncle, he was the colored overseer, he went to Danbury, six miles from whar we lived at, and he paid $5 for a pound of coffee. Dat was befo de North whupped de South, and dey had'n killed-down de money value for de South."

"Talk about hard times! We see'd em in dem days, durin' de war and most specially after de Surrender. Folks dese days dont know what trouble looks like. We was glad to eat ash-cakes and drink parched corn and rye 'stead o coffee. I've seed my grandmother go to de smoke house, and scrape up de dirt whar de meat had drapped, and take it to de house fer seasonin. You see, both armies fed off'n de white folks, and dey cleaned out dey barns and cellars and smoke houses when dey come. One time, when de Yanks was on de way to Augusta, I was picking up chips to make the supper fire, when I see'd em comin'. I hit it out from dar and hide behind two little hills down by de big spring. After awhile my brother find me and he tell me to come on back to the house and see dem white mens dance. De Yanks kep' comin' and dey eat all night. By daylight they was through marchin past."

"An den come de Rebels. When dey come we had five-thousand bushel of corn, one-hundred head o hogs, three-hundred and fifty galons of syrup 'en sech. When dey left, they took an set fire to evything, to keep it away from the Yanks, aimin to starve em out o dat country. Dat's what dey done. Some of dem Rebs was mean as the Yanks. And dat was bein' mean. Some called de Yanks, 'de Hornets', 'cause dey fight so. Take a Yank an he'd fight acrost a buzz saw and it circlin' fifty mile a minute."

"Dat time when the Yanks was goin' to Augusta, an I went to black my Marster's boot,—he'd give us a two-cent peice, big as a quarter—for boot blackin, I say, 'Marster who is dem soldiers?' An he say to me, 'Dey's de Yankees, come to try to take you awy from me.' An I say, 'Looks like to me Marster, ef'n dey wants to take us dey'd arsk you fer us.' Marster laughed and say, 'Boy! Dem fellers dont axes wid words. Dey does all dey talkin' wid cannons.' Did you know that a white woman shot de first cannon dat was ever fired in de state o Georgia? She was a Yankee Colonel's wife, dey say, named Miss Anna, I dunno the rest o her name. She wants to be de first to fire a cannon she say, to set the negroes free. Dat was befo' de war, begin. De roar of dat cannon was in folkes ears for more'n five days and nights."

Uncle Andrew gave a little grunt as he lifted himself out of his chair. His little frame seemed lost in the broad-shouldered lumber jacket that he wore. He had laid aside the paper sack from which he had been eating, when the visitor came, and removed an old stocking cap from his head. When the visitor suggested that he keep it on, as he might catch cold he replied, "I dont humor myself none." The sunlight fell upon his head and shoulders as he stood, to steady himself on his feet. Traces of his ancestry of Indian blood,—one of his grandfathers was a Cherokee Indian,—were evident in his features. His skin is jet-black, but his forehead high and his nose straight, with nostrils only slightly full. There was dignity in his bearing and beauty in his face, with its halo of cotton-white hair and beard, cut short and neatly parted in the middle of his chin.

Walking about the room, he called the visitor's attention to family portraits on the walls. Some were colored crayons, and a few were enlarged snap-shots. Proudly he pointed to the photograph of a huge-sized Negro man, apparently in his thirties, and said, "He was our first comins'. Reckon he took after his great granddaddy, who was eight feet tall and weighed twe-hundred and fifty pounds. That man's arms was so long, when dey hung down by his side, his fingers was below his knees. Dis grandfather was free-born. My father, Dave Moss, he was sold three times. He had twenty-five children. But he had two wives. As I aforesaid, folks didn't always marry in dem days, jes took up wid one another. My mother was his title-wife. By her, he jes had me and my two full-brothers an one sister. My mother died two years after de war. My father give my sister to my grandmother. Jes give 'er to 'er."

"How come I live in Knoxville, I was a young man, when I started off from Georgia, aimin to go over de mountains to Kentucky whar I heard dey pay good wages. I stopped in Campbell country, Tennessee wid another feller, an' I see'd a pretty gal workin' in de field. An I say's, I'm goin' to marry dat gal. Sho 'nough me an her was married in less dan six months. Her Marster build us a log house and we lived dar 'till we come to Knoxville, Tennessee. Now, all o my boys is dead. Evy one o em worked for Mr. Peters (Peters and Bradley Flour Mills, of Knoxville)—and dey all died workin' fer him. So Mister Willie, he say he gwine let me live here, in de company house, the rest o my days."

The four room frame house stands near a creek at the dead end of an alley on which both whites and negroes live. The huge double bed, neatly made, stands between two windows from which there is an unobstructed view of the highway traversing north and south through northern Knoxville, several blocks away from Andrew's home. "I jes lay down on dat bed nights and watch them autimobiles flyin by. Dey go Blip! Blip! and Blip! An I say to my self, 'Watch them fools!' Folkes ain got de sense dey's born wid. Ain smart like dey used to be. An times ain good like dey was. Ef'n it hadnt been for some of dem crazy fools, actin up and smarty, me an my wife'd be gittin maybe a hun'ered an' more dollars a month, 'stead o the fifteen we gits 'tween us for ole' age help. They'd ought to let Rosevelt alone. An its his own folks as is fitin' 'im. He is a big man even ef he is a Democrat. I'm a Republican though. Voted my first time for Blaine."

"Yes I votes sometimes now, when dey come gits me. An befo I got sick, I would ride the street car to town. An I goes down to de Court House, and when I see dem cannons in deyard I cain keep from cryin'. My wife arsk me what make me go look at dem cannon ef'n dey makes me cry. An I tells her I cry 'bout de good and de bad times dem cannon bringed us. But no cannons or nothin' else, seems like going to bring back de good old times. But I dont worry 'bout all dese things much. Accordin' to de Good Book's promise, weepin' may endure for a night, den come joy in de mornin. An I knows dat de day's soon come when I goes to meet my folks and my Lord an Marster in his Heaven, whar dey ain no more weepin.'"

SUBJECT—EX-SLAVE STORIES

AUNT MOLLIE MOSS
88- Auburn Street,
Knoxville, Tennessee

There is no street sign or a number on any of the ramshackled frame cottages that seemingly lean with the breezes, first one direction, then another, along the alley that wind's through the city's northernmost boundary and stops its meanderings at the doorstep of "Uncle Andrew Moss" and his wife, "Aunt Mollie."

TENNESSEE NARRATIVES

The City Directory of Knoxville, Tennessee officially lists the Moss residence as # 88 Auburn Street. It rests upon its foundations more substantially, and is in better kept condition than its neighbors. In lieu of a "reg'lar" house number, the aged negro couple have placed a rusty automobile lisence tag of ancient vintage conspicuously over their door. It is their jesture of contempt for their nearest white neighbors who "dont seem to care whedder folkses know whar dey lib an maybe don wants em to."

As for Aunt Mollie, she holds herself superior to all of her neighbors. She "Ain got no time for po white trash noway." She shoo'ed two little tow-headed white girls from her doorstep with her broom as she stood in her door and watched a visitor approach. "G'wan way frum here now, can be bodder wid you chillun messin ups my front yard. Take yo tings an go on back to yo own place!"

"Dats way dey do," she mummled as she lead the visitor inside the cottage, through the dining-room and kitchen into the living-room and bedroom. "Don know what I gwine do when come summer time. Keeps me all time lookin out for dem chilluns. Dey's dat troublesome. Brings trash in on my flo what I jes scoured, an musses 'roun, maybe tryin to steal sumpin an me watchin em too. Dey wasnt teached manners and 'havior in odder folkses houses like what I war."

When Aunt Mollie learned that it was to hear her story of how she was trained in manners end behaviorism, that the visitor had come, and to hear something of her recollections of slave days, her belligerent mood vanished. The satisfied manner in which she drew up chairs before the fire, took a pinch of snuff and settled her skirts, indicated that was going to be quite a session. She leaned her elbows on her knees, held her head between the palms of her hands and fumbled in her cloudy memory to gather a few facts to relate.

Uncle Andrew, the more intelligent of the two, and quick to seize upon his opportunity, began his reminiscences immediately, saying "Honey, wait now," when his wife thought herself well organized to talk, and frequently broke into his narrative. "Wait untell I gits through. Den you can talk." Aunt Mollie would frown and grunt, mumble to herself as she rocked back and forth in her chair. She pulled the two long braids of brown silky hair, streaked with white, and tied at the ends with cotton strings. She spat vigorously into the fire, kept muttering and shuffling her feet, which were encased in men's shoes.

At last it came Aunt Mollie's turn to talk war-times. Uncle Andrew, well pleased with his recital, retired to his corner by the hearth and listened "mannerdly"—after first warning the visitor in a gentle undertone, that "My wife she ain got much mem'ry an she don hear good." Aunt Mollie's rambling reminiscences backed up his statement. She began.

"Reckon I mus be 'bout eighty-two, three year old. I dunno exactly. Ef I knowed whar to find em, deys some my white folkes lib in dis town. Seem like I can 'member dey names. I b'longed to Marster Billy Cain, and was raised on his farm in Campbell county, Tennessee. Oh, 'bout six, seven mile from Jacksboro. Wish I could go back dar some time. Ain been dar sence me an Moss married an live eight, ten or some more years in a log cabin he built for us. We was married March 7, de day atter Cleveland was 'lected president. In 1885 did you say? Well, reckon you're right. I ain had no schoolin an I can 'member lots o tings I used to know."

"Billy Cain worked me in de fields. An his wife Miss Nancy say she gwine stop it, 'cause I was so pretty she fraid somebody come steal me." Aunt Mollie buried her face in her apron and had a good laugh. "Dey said I was de pretties' girl anywhars about. Had teeth jes like pearls. Whoops! Look at em now. Ain got 'nuff left to chaw wid. You notices how light-complected I is? My own father was a full-blooded Cherokee Indian. De Yanks captured him an killed him."

"I was hoein in de field dat time Moss com 'long and see me and say he gwine marry me. An, jes like he tell you, we was married in less dan six months. We been livin togedder evy since and we gits along good. We have had blessins' and got a lot to be thankful for. Could have more to eat sometimes, but we gits along someways. I am a good cook. Miss Nancy she teached me all kinds o cookin, puttin up berries, makin pickles and bakin bread and cake an evy'ting. Her ole man Cain give us good grub dem days. Monday mornins' we go to de Cains to git rations for de week. Dey gib us three pounds wheat, a peck o meal, a galon o molasses, two pound o lard, two pound o brown sugar, rice an evy'ting. I use to have plates an china white folks gib me. White woman come one day, say she wan buy 'em. Took plum nigh all I had. Did'n pay me much o nothin' either."

"Yes, Lord. I does 'member 'bout de war. I've see'd de blue an I've see'd de grey. In 1862 I see'd de soldiers formin' in line. I was a great big girl. Dem swords glisen' like stars. Can' member whar dey was goin dat time. But I ain forgit de times soldiers come foragin. Dey got all dey wanted, too. Hep' dey sef's an dont pay for it, never. Soldier see a chicken go under de house, he plop down and shoot, and den call me to crawl under de house and fetch it out." Aunt Mollie buried her head in her apron again and laughed like a child. "Lordy how scared I was of de old gander dat blowed at me, whilst I was tryin' to drag 'em out alive, when I see'd de soldiers comin'."

"Billy Cain, he was brudder-in-law to Old Townslee, who lived on a plantation in Alabama. How come my mother was give to Cain an come to Tennessee, was one mornin' Old Townslee rode his horse out under a tree to blow up de slaves. Blow de horn you know, to call 'em to work. Somebody shot 'im. Right off his horse. It was so dark, 'fore daylight, an' couldnt see and dey never did find out who shot 'im. Heap o white folks had enemies dem days. So de slaves he owned was divided munxt his chilluns. My mother was one of nine dat come to Billy Cain dat way."

"Talk 'bout your shootin jest for devilment. Lemme tell you 'bout old men John Wynn. He live down dar 'bout ten mile from whar Moss lived when he was a boy. I've heard em tell it many a time. Dey say John Wynn had 185 slaves. Evy time it come George Washington's birthday, Old Wynn he had a feast and invite all de slaves! He celebratin! he say. He seta a long table wid all kind good tings to eat. An he count de slaves, so's to be sure dey all come. An' den he'd take an pick out one and shoot him! Den he say, "Now youse all can go 'head an eat. Throw dat nigger 'side an we bury im in mornin'." And he walks off to de big house. No! He wasn't drunk. Jes de debil in 'im. Well, he shot ten, twelve, maybe thirty dat way. An den de white folks hanged 'im to a tree. Hanged im t'well he was good and dead, dey did."

"Now folkes can 'joy dey victuals wid sech goin's on. De slaves git so's dey scared to hear de bell ring. Don' know what it mean. Maybe death, maybe fire, maybe nudder sale o some body. Gwine take 'em way. But when de bell ring dey had to come. Let dat ole bell ring and de woods was full o negroes. Maybe 500 hundred come from all over date county."

Aunt Mollie was beginning to ramble and babble incoherently, her memories of her own and the experiences of others all confused in her mind. When she had about finished a story about how one of the slave women, "bust de skull" of the head of her marster,'" 'cause she was nussin a sick baby an' he tell her she got to git out in dat field an hoe" and the gory details of what the shovel did to the white marster's head, it was time for the visitors to close the interview.

Both Uncle Andrew and Aunt Mollie followed the visitor to the front door, and wished her "All de luck in de world. An thank you for comin'. An come see us agin, nudder time."

INTERVIEW: ANDY ODELL
1313 Pearl Street
Nashville, Tennessee

"I wuz bawn east ob Spring Hill, Tennessee. I dunno in w'at y'ar, but I wuz a ful' grown man w'en I wuz freed. (This will make him about 96 years old.). I wuz an onlies' chile en I nebber knowed mah daddy. Mah mammy wuz sold 'way fum me. She ma'ied a man named Brown en dey had seven chillun."

"At fust I 'longed ter Marster Jim Caruthers. W'en his daughter ma'ied Fount Odell, I wuz willed ter her en den mah marsters wuz Fount en Albert Odell who wuz br'ers. Mah white folks let us go ter chuch. I b'leeves in de Baptist 'ligion. I nebber knowed any slave dat had ter hide ter sing er pray. I members de comet en hit wuz a sta'r wid a long tail en looked lak hit wuz burnin'. De sta'rs fell 'fore I wuz bawn." (The stars fell in 1833).

"We had ter hab passes en if you didn't hab one, you got whupped. Mah marster let me go ter chuch wid' out a pass. I members de Klu Klux Klan but dey nebber bothered me, tho I 'yeard a lot 'bout dem. Dey called demselves "White Caps" en said dey wuz rite fum de grave. W'en a slave got whupped hit wuz cose dey disobey dere white folks en de overseer whupped dem. I though mah white folks wuz awful mean ter me sumtime."

"I nebber b'leeved in ghos' but hab yeard lots 'bout dem. Lots of peeples did b'leeve in dem back in dem times. Uster sing a lot but I dunno names ob dem now. I dunno w'at ez gwine ter 'kum ob dis young crowd. I sho don't think diff'ent culers oughter ma'rie. De Lawd didn't mean fer hit ter be dun. Dunno ob any slave 'risin's in Virginia er any uther place. Don't member now de tales en sayin' ob de ole times."

"Member well w'en de war broke out en how dey had big dinners en marched 'round ovuh de fiel's, gittin' ready fer de war. I had a br'er kilt in de war en mah mammy got a lettle money fum 'im. Also member dat w'en mah mammy got de money she bought me a hat."

"I don't git nuthin at freedum en I dunno ob any slaves gittin' any land er money. I know dat w'en we wuz freed Marster Albert called us slaves in en said, "You all ez as free as I ez, but you can stay 'yer en wuk fer me ef'n you want ter." I staid wid 'im a good w'ile attar freedum."

"Since freedum I hab plowed, hoed, cut wood, en wuk'd in quarries pecking rock. Hab nebber wuk'd in town fer I dunno de things 'bout town. I hab voted almost eve'y election since freedum 'til dese last few years. I hab had two frens in office but both ez de'd now. I uster think 'omen shouldn't vote, but I guess hit ez alri'te."

TENNESSEE NARRATIVES

INTERVIEW: LAURA RAMSEY PARKER
715 Gay St.
Nashville, Tennessee

"I'se 87 y'ars ole. Wuz bawn in slavery. Wuz freed w'en de slavery stopped. Mack Ramsey wuz mah marster en he wuz sho good ter his slaves. He treated dem as human bein's. W'en he turned his slaves 'loose he gib dem no money, but gib dem lands, clothin' en food 'til dey could brang in dere fust crop. Mah daddy rented a strip ob land 'til he wuz able ter buy de place. He lived on de same fer menny y'ars."

"W'en I wuz ole er'nuff I wuz taught ter spin en weav. I bucum de nuss ter de marster's onlies' chile. Soon atter I wuz freed, I went ter Wisconsin, but only wuz dere fer a y'ar, den I kum back ter Tennessee en Nashville. I settled in dis house en I'se bin livin' in hit fer ovuh fifty y'ars. Dere wuz no uther houses 'round 'yer at de time. I own de place. Hab wuk'd all mah life seem ter me. At one time I wuz a chambermaid at de Nicholson House now de Tulane en later 'kum a sick nuss, a seamstress, dressmaker but now I pieces en sells bed quilts. I does mah own housekeepin' en washin'."

"I don't member now, very much 'bout de Ku Klux Klan. I do member dat one nite dey passed our home en I grab'ed a shotgun en said dat I wuz gwine ter shoot dem ef dey kum on de place. I members de Battle ob Murfreesboro, but I'se got no membrances ob any slave uprisin'."

"I think very lettle ob de younger ginerashon. Dere's many things ter day dat should be changed, but I'se 'yer en can't do nuthin' ter change hit. I's min'in mah own business. I puts mah faith en trust in Gawd's han's; en treats mah nabers right; en lives honest. I 'longs ter de Christian Chuch, but don't wan'ter be called a "Campbellite.""

"De songs I members ez:

Am I a Soldier ob de Cross.
 Am I Bawn ter Die?
 'Tis 'Ligion Dat Can Gib."

INTERVIEW: NAISY REECE
710 Overton St.
Nashville, Tennessee

"I wuz bawn in slavery, in Williamson County, guess I'se 'bout 80 y'ars ole. Think I wuz fou' w'en de wah started."

"Mah mammy en daddy wuz Mary en Ennock Brown."

"Mah missis en marster wuz Polly en Randall Brown."

"Dunno ob any ob our fam'ly bein' sold. W'en freedum wuz declar' we wuz tu'n loose wid nothin'. Mah daddy tuk us down in de kuntry, raised crops en made us wuk in de fiel'."

"I'se cooked a leetle fer urther peeple, but mos' ob mah wuk has bin laundry. I didn't go ter schul much. I dunno w'at ter say 'bout de younger gineratshun; dere ez sich a diff'unce now ter w'at hit wuz w'en I wuz a girl. Dunno any tales dat I useter 'year."

"Didn't see any Klu Klux Klan, but I alluz got skeered en hid w'en we'd 'year dey wuz kumin'. I 'long ter de Baptist Church. I neber went ter menny camp-meetin's, but went ter a lot ob baptizins."

"Mammy tole us how de sta'rs fell en how skeered eberybody got. I saw de long tail comet."

Signs: "Good luck ter git up 'fore day-lite ef'n youer gwin sum place er start sum wuk." "Bad luck ter sweep flo' atter dark en sweep de dirt out."

Songs: "I Couldn't Hear Anybody Pray."
"Ole Time 'Ligion."
"Cross De Riber Jordan."

"I'se neber voted, en hab neber had any frens in office. Neber knowed nothin' 'bout de slave mart er de 'structshun days."

INTERVIEW: MILLIE SIMPKINS
"BLACK MAMIE"
1004 10th Avenue, No.
Nashville, Tennessee

I claims I's 109 ye'ars ole en wuz bawn neah Winchester, Tennessee. Mah marster wuz Boyd Sims en mah missis wuz Sarah Ann Ewing Sims. Mah mammy wus named Judy Ewing en mah daddy wuz Moses Stephens en he wus "free bawn." He wuz de marster's stable boy en followed de races. He run 'way en nebber kum back.

Mah fust missis wuz very rich. She had two slave 'omen ter dress her eve'y mawnin' en I brought her breakfust ter her on a silvah waitah. She wuz ma'ied three times, her second husband wuz Joe Carter en de third wuz Judge Gork.

Mah fust missis sold me kaze I wuz stubborn. She sent me ter de "slave yard" at Nashville. De yard wuz full ob slaves. I stayed dere two weeks 'fore marster Simpson bought me. I wuz sold 'way fum mah husband en I nebber se'd 'im 'gin. I had one chile which I tuk wid me.

De slave yard wuz on Cedar Street. A Mr. Chandler would bid de slaves off, but 'fore dey started biddin' you had ter tek all ob yo Clothes off en roll down de hill so dey could see dat you didn't hab no bones broken, er sores on yer. (I wouldin' tek mine off). Ef nobody bid on you, you wuz tuk ter de slave mart en sold. I wuz sold dere. A bunch ob dem wuz sent ter Mississippi en dey had dere ankles fas'end tergedder en dey had ter walk w'iles de tradahs rid.

W'en I wuz sold ter marster Simpkins, mah second mistress made me a house slave en I wuked only at de big house en mah wuk wus ter nuss en dress de chilluns en he'ps mah missis in her dressin'.

De young slaves wuz hired out ter nuss de white chilluns. I wuz hired as nuss girl at seven y'ars ole en started cookin' at ten. I nebber had a chance ter go ter schul.

I'm de mammy ob 14 chilluns, seven boys en seven gals. I wuz next ter de olest ob four chillun. Mah missis useter hire me out ter hotels en taverns.

Sum marsters fed dare slaves meat en sum wouldin' let dem hab a bite. One marster we useter 'yer 'bout would grease his slaves mouth on Sunday mawnin', en tell dem ef any body axed ef dey had meat ter say "yes, lots ob hit".

W'en dey got ready ter whup dem dey'd put dem down on a pit widout any clothes, stand back wid a bull whup en cut de blood out. I member de niggers would run 'way en hide out.

De only fun de young folks had wuz w'en de ole folks had a quiltin'. W'ile de ole folks wuz wukin' on de quilt de young ones would git in 'nuther room, dance en hab a good time. Dey'd hab a pot turned down at de do'er ter keep de white folks fum 'yearin' dem. De white folks didn't want us ter l'arn nothin' en ef a slave picked up a lettle piece ob papah, dey would yell "put dat down you—you wan't ter git in our business."

De white folks wouldin' let de slaves pray, ef dey got ter pray hit wuz w'iles walkin' 'hind de plow. White folks would whup de slaves ef dey 'yeard dem sing er pray.

I wuz a big girl w'en dey build de Capitol. I played on de hill 'fore hit wuz built en I toted blocks fum dere w'en hit wuz bein' built. I wuz livin' in Dickson County w'en Fort Donelson wuz tuk. I seed de fust gun boat dat kum up de Cumberland River. I wuz standin' in de Do'er w'en I se'd hit kumin', but hit didn't tek me long ter git back in de back ob de house. I wuz skeered dey would shoot.

Mah marster run a fer'y en atter de gun boat kum up de riber, he got skeered en gib mah ole man de fer'y, en w'en de soldiers kum ter tek Fort Negley he set dem 'cross de river.

A man at Ashland City dat made whisk'y would hab Mr. Simpkins bring a load ob logs up ter Ashland City en den bring a load ob whiskey down en hide hit so de Yankees would'nt git hit.

Mah marster had a fish trap at de mouth ob Harper en w'en de gun boat passed dey shot thro' de trap.

I wuz right 'yer w'en de Civil wah wuz gwin on, en de soldiers wuz dressed up en beatin' de drums.

No honey we didn't git nothin' w'en we wuz freed. Jes druv 'way widout nothin' ter do wid. We got in a waggin en druv ter nuther man's plantashun. Mah ole man made a crap dere. Sum ob de slaves might hab got sump'in but I dunno nobody dat did. I wuz skeered ter op'n mah do'er atter dark on 'count ob Ku Klux Klan, dey wuz red hot.

I member w'en de sta'rs fell. I wuz small but de ole folks run out en looked at dem, kum back set down en cried, dey tho't hit me'nt de worl' wuz kumin' ter an end.

De peeple wuz skeered w'en dey se'd de comet wid de long tail. Dey tho't hit wuz a sign ob wah.

I'se cooked eve'y since I wuz freed. I stayed in Henry Galbles kitchen five long y'ars, en since I'se had dese strokes hit's broke me up 'till I kin do nothin'. I 'long ter de Methodist Church. I think de young peeples ez turrible, en dis white en black mar'iags not be 'lowed.

De songs I member ez:

"Dark wuz de Night".
 "Good Ole Daniel".

I'se nebber voted but I'se electioneered fer dem. Hab nebber had any frens in office.

I wuz 'yer w'en Henry Clay en James K. Polk wuz runnin'. I wuz hired at de ole City Hotel ovuh on de river. I wuz din'in room servant dere. Mah marster would hab me sing a song fer him 'bout de Democrats. "Hooray de kuntry ez risin'; rise up en drown ole Clay en his pizen". I guess ole Clay wuz a right good fellow but he played cards wid de niggers in de cellar.

De only thing I member 'bout de 'structshun time wuz sum ob de whites didn't wan' de niggers ter vote.

I stays 'yer wid mah daughter. Dat ez de only support I hab since I had deze strokes en bin unable ter do fer mahse'f.

TENNESSEE NARRATIVES

EX-SLAVE STORIES

SUBJECT: JOSEPH LEONIDAS STAR,
133 Quebec Place,
Knoxville, Tennessee

If the poetic strain in the Dunbar Negroes of the south is an inheritance and not "just a gift from On High," Knoxville, Tennessee's aged Negro Poet,—born Joseph Leonidas Star,—but prominently known in the community as "Lee" Star, Poet, Politician and Lodge Man,—thinks that Georgia's poetic genius Paul Lawrence Dunbar, "maybe took his writin' spells" from him.

"My grandfather and Paul Lawrence Dunbar's grandfather was cousins. He were a much younger man than I am, for I was eighty-one years old the twenty-sixth of December, 1937. So I reckon I give it down to my kin-man. But it seem to me, that Poets is just born thataway. Po'try is nothin' but Truth anyway, and it's Truth was sets us free. And that makes me a free-born citizen bothways and every ways. I were born free. I were always happy-natured and I expect to die thataway. One of my poems is named, 'Be Satisfied!' and I say in it that if a man's got somethin' to eat, and teeth to bite, he should be satisfied. You cant take your goods with you. Old man Rockefeller, when he died here awhile back, went away from here 'thout his hat and shoes. That's the way its goin' to be with all us, no matter what our color is."

"The people 'round here calls me "Lee" Star, and I want to tell you, Lee Star is a free-born man. But of course, things bein' as they were, both my mother and father were slaves. That is for a few years. They lived in Greenville, Tennessee. My mother, Maria Guess, was free'd before the emancipation, by the good words of her young white mistress, who told 'me [TR: 'em] all when she was about to die, she wanted 'em to set Maria free, 'cause she didn't want her little playmate to be nobodys else's slave. They was playmates you see. My mother was eleven years old when she was freed."

"When she was about fourteen and my father Henry Dunbar wanted to marry he had to first buy his freedom. In them times a slave couldn't marry a free'd person. So he bought his freedom from his Marster Lloyd Bullen, and a good friend of Andrew Johnson, the presi-dent. My father an' him was friends too. So he bought his freedom, for just a little of somethin' I disremember what, 'cause they didn't aim to make him buy his freedom high. He made good money though. He was a carpenter, blacksmith, shoe maker and knowed a lot more trades. His Master was broadhearted, and good to his slaves, and he let 'em work at anything they want to, when they was done their part of white folks chore-work."

"Both my father and mother was learned in the shoe makin' trade. When they come to Knoxville to live, and where I was born, they had a great big shoe shop out there close to where Governor Brownlow lived. Knoxville just had three streets, two runnin' east and west and one run north and south. I well remember when General Burnside come to Knoxville. That was endurin' the siege of Knoxville. Before he marched his men out to the Battle of Fort Saunders, he stopped his solider [TR: soldier] band in front of our shoe shop and serenaded my mother and father. I was a little boy and I climed up on the porch bannisters and sat there and lissen' to that music."

"I remember another big man come here once when I was a boy and I served the transient trade at a little eatin' place right where the Atkin Ho-tel is now. Jeff Davis come there to eat, when he stopped over between trains. That was in 1869. No, I disremember what he eat or how he behave. He didnt seem no different from any other man. He was nince lookin' wore a long tail coat and his boots was plenty blacked. He favored pictures of Abraham Lincoln. Was about middle-height and had short, dark chin-whiskers. I were very busy at the time, an' if they was any excitement I didnt know it."

"Yes, I've seen many a slave in my day. One of my boy playmates was a slave child. His name is Sam Rogan and he lives now at the County Poor Farm. I make it a point not to dwell too much on slave times. I was learned different. I've had considerable schoolin', went to my first school in the old First Presbyterian church. My teachers was white folks from the North. They give us our education and give us clothes and things sent down here from the North. That was just after the surrender. I did see a terrible sight once. A slave with chains on him as long as from here to the street. He was in an ole' buggy, settin' between two white men and they was passin' through Knoxville. My mother and father wouldnt lissen' to me tell 'em about it when I got home. And I hope I forget everything I ever knowed or heard about salves [TR: slaves], and slave times."

Joseph Leonidas Star, no longer works at the shoemakers trade. He writes poetry and lives leisurely in a three room frame shanty, in a row of shabbier ones that face each other disconsolately on a typical Negro alleyway, that has no shade trees and no paving. "Lee's" house is the only one that does not wabble uneasily, flush with the muddy alley. His stands on a small brick foundation, a few feet behind a privet hedge in front, with a brick wall along the side in which he has cemented a few huge conch shells.

After fifty-four years residence here, a political boss in his ward, and the only Negro member of the Young White Men's Republican League, Star's influence in his community is attested by the fact that when he "destructed", the Knoxville City Council to "please do somethin' about it, Knoxville being too big a city to keep callin' street's alleys," the City Council promptly and unanimously voted to change the name of King's Alley to Quebec Place.

When the interviewer called, Star's door was padlocked. But he appeared soon, having received word by the grape-vine system that some one "was to see him",—"They told me it was the Sherriff" he laughed. He came down the long muddy alley at a lively clip. He claimes he is able to walk about 20 miles each day, just to keep in condition. He wore a broad-brimmed black "derby-hat", a neatly pressed serge suit in two tones, a soiled white pleated shirt and a frazzled-edged black bow tie. His coat lapels and vest-front were adorned with badges and emblems, including his Masonic pins, a Friendship Medal, his Republican button and a silver crucifix. The Catholic church, according to Lee, is the only one in Knoxville which permits the black man to worship under the same roof with his white brothers.

Many of Star's poems have been published in the local and state papers. He keeps a record of deaths of all citizens, and has done so for sixty years. He calls the one, which records murders and hanging, his "Doomsday Book", and "encoached" in it he claims is an accurate date record of all such events of importance in his lifetime. His records are neatly inscribed in a printing form and very legible. His conversation is marked by grammatical incongruities, but he does not speak the Negro dialect.

INTERVIEW: DAN THOMAS
941 Jefferson Street
Nashville, Tennessee

"I wuz bawn in slavery in 1847 at Memphis, Tennessee en mah marster wuz Deacon Allays. Mah mammy wuz de cook at de big house. Mah mammy d'ed soon atter I wuz bawn, en de Missis had me raised on a bottle. Marster en Missis treatus all dere slaves kindly en plenty ter eat en eve'y one wuz happy. I dunno nuthin 'bout mah daddy er whar he went. I hab no kin in dis worl'. All I eber yeard wuz dat all mah folks kum fum Africa. Mah Missis would tell me dat I mus' be good en mine en eberbody will lak' you en ef she d'ed, dey would tek keer ob me. Dat ez w'at dey hab don."

"I wuked 'round de house 'tel I wuz 'bout ten y'ars ole en de Marster put me ter wuk in his big whiskey house. W'en I got 'bout 21 y'ars ole, I would go out ter collect bills fum Marster's customers en hit tuk me 'bout a week ter git all 'round. I wuzn't 'lowed ter tek money but had ter git dere checks. I also wuked 18 y'ars as bar tender. Marster en Mistress d'ed 'bout four y'ars 'fore whiskey went out ob de United States. I stay wid dem 'til dey d'ed."

"Atter de Marster en Missis d'ed de doctor sezs I would hab ter leave Memphis on 'count ob my health. I kum ter Nashville en got a job at de "Powder Plant" durin' de Worl' War, en stayed dere 'til hit wuz ovuh. I den gets wuk at Foster en Creighton in Nashville 'till dey tole me dat I wuz too ole ter wuk. I makes mah livin' now by haulin' slop en pickin' up things dat de white folks throw in dere trash pile en sum ob hit I sell ter de papah en junk dealers. De white peeple he'p me now also."

TENNESSEE NARRATIVES

"I se'd dem sell a lot ob slaves in Mississippi, jes' lak hosses en hogs, one time w'en de Marster en Mistress made a trip down dere. Lots ob times dey made trips 'round de kuntry en dey allus tuk me 'long. I se'd sum cru'l Marsters dat hitched up dere slaves ter plows en made dem plow lak hosses en mules did."

"Atter de slaves got dere freedum, dey had ter look atter demselves, so dey would wuk on plantations till dey got so dey could rent a place, lak you rent houses en farms terday. Sum got places whar dey wuk'd fer wages."

"I voted three times in mah life but lawdy dat wuz a long time ago. I voted fer Teddy Roosevelt en Woodrow Wilson, en mah last vote wuz 'bout two y'ars pas'."

"Hab no tales handed down by mah peeple. W'en I would try ter git info'mation, atter I got o'ler, all dey would say wuz, "You wuz raised on a bottle en hab no peeple ob you own."

"Oh mah goodness! Hit jes par'lises me ter see how dem young peeple ez doin' terday. Lawdy hab mercy but dere ez as much diff'ent fum ole times as day en nite en hit looks lak things hab gone astray. Wuz tole lots 'bout de Ku Klux Klan en how dey would catch en whup de cul'ed peeple, but mah white folks made me stay in en dey neber got me."

"I member seein' Andrew Jackson, General Grant en Abraham Lincoln, member seein' General Andrew Jackson git'in ready fer war by marchin' his soldiers erroun'. I se'd 'im ride his big white hoss up en down ter see how dey marched."

"One song I lack'd best ob all wuz, 'Mah ole Mammy ez De'd en Gon',' 'Let me Sit B'neath de Willow Tree.' Don't member uther songs now."

INTERVIEW: SYLVIA WATKINS
411 14th Avenue N.
Nashville, Tennessee.

I'se said ter be 91 y'ars ole. I wuz young w'en de War wuz goin' on. I wuz bawn in Bedford County. Mah mammy wuz named Mariah. She had six chillun by mah daddy en three by her fust husband.

Mah missis wuz named Emily Hatchet en de young missises wuz Mittie en Bettie, dey wuz twins. We had good clothes ter w'ar en w'en we went ter de table hit wuz loaded wid good food en we could set down en eat our stomachs full. Oh Lawd I wish dem days wuz now so I'd hab sum good food. Ob course, we had ter wuk in de fiel's en mek w'at we et.

Wen we'd finish our day's wuk our missis would let us go out en play hide en seek, Puss in de corner, en diff'ent games.

Mah mammy wuz sold in Virginia w'en she wuz a gurl. She sezs 'bou 60 ob em wuz put in de road en druv down 'yer by a slave trader, lak a bunch ob cattle. Mah mammy en two ob mah sistahs wuz put on a block, sold en carried ter Alabama. We neber 'yeard fum dem nomo', en dunno whar dey ez.

I wuz willed ter mah young missis w'en she ma'ried. I wuz young en, ob course, she whuped me, but she wasn't mean ter me. I needed eve'y whupin' she eber gib me, cause I wuz allus fightin'. Mah missis allus called me her lettle nig.

Mah daddy could only see mah mammy Wednesday en Saturday nites, en ef'n he kum wid'out a pass de pat-rollers would whup 'im er run 'im 'til his tongue hung out. On dem nites we would sit up en look fer daddy en lots ob times he wuz out ob bref cose he had run so much.

Mah white folks had a loom en we wove our own clothes. I wuz nuss en house girl en l'arned how ter sew en nit. Mah young missis wuz blind 'fore she died. I useter visit her once a Ye'r en she'd load me down wid things ter tek home, a linsey petticoat, ham bones, cracklins en diff'ent things. She died 18 years ago almos' a 100 ye'r ole.

De white folks wouldn't let de slaves hab a book er papah fer fear dey'd l'arn sumpin', en ef dey wan'ed ter pray dey'd tu'n a kettle down at dere cabin do'er. I member yearin' mah mammy pray "Oh Father op'n up de do'ers en sho us lite." I'd look up ter de ceiling ter see ef he wuz gonna op'n up sumpin'; silly, silly me, thinkin' such. I's 'longs ter de Missionary Baptist chuch but I don't git ter go very off'n.

I wuz tole 'fore freedum dat de slaves would git a mule, land en a new suit, but our missis didn't gib us a thing. She promis' me, mah br'rer, en three sistahs ef'n we would stay wid her a ye'r, en he'p her mek a crop she would gib us sump'in ter start us a crop on w'en we lef' her.

Mah daddy's marster wus named Bob Rankin, he gib mah daddy a hog, sum chickens, let him hab a cow ter milk en land ter raise a crop on. He wan'ed mah daddy ter git us tergedder ter he'p daddy raise a crop but since mah missis had promised us so much, daddy let us stay wid her a ye'r. On de nite mah daddy kum fer us, mah missis sezs I've not got nuthin ter gib you, fer I won't hab nobody ter do nuthin fer me. We went wid our daddy. We lived dere on Marster Rankin's farm fer ye'rs in fact so long we tho't de place 'longed ter mah daddy. We had a house wid big cracks in hit, had a big fier place, a big pot dat hong on de fier en a skillet dat we cooked corn bread in. Had a hill ob taters under de house, would raise up a plank, rake down in de dirt git taters, put dem in de fier ter roast. We had meat ter eat in de middle ob de day but none at mawnin' er nite. We got one pair ob shoes a ye'r, dey had brass on de toes. I uster git out en shine de toes ob mine, we called hit gol' on our shoes. We wuked in de fiel' wid mah daddy, en I know how ter do eberting dere ez ter do in a fiel' 'cept plow, I wuz allus ter slender ter hold a plow. We had grease lamps. A thing lak a goose neck wid platted rag wick in hit. Would put grease in hit.

Durin' slavery ef one marster had a big boy en 'nuther had a big gal da marsters made dem libe tergedder. Ef'n de 'oman didn't hab any chilluns, she wuz put on de block en sold en 'nuther 'oman bought. You see dey raised de chilluns ter mek money on jes lak we raise pigs ter sell.

Mah mammy tole me 'bout de sta'rs fallin' en den I se'ed de second fallin' ob sta'rs. Dey didn't hit de groun' lak de fust did. I member de comet hit had a long tail. I lef' mah daddy en kum ter Nashville wid missis Nellie Rankin, (daddy's young missus) in 1882; hab bin 'yer eber since. I'se dun house wuk fer a lot ob peeples. Kep house fer a 'oman in Belle Meade fer 14 ye'rs. Now I'se aint able ter do nothin. I'se bin ma'ried twice. Ma'ried Jimm Ferguson, libed wid 'im 20 ye'ars he d'ed. Two ye'ars later I mar'ed George Watkins, lived wid him 8 ye'ars; two ye'ars ago he died. I'se neber had any chilluns. I kep wan'in ter 'dopt a lettle gal, de fust husban' wouldn't do hit. 'Bout 5-1/2 ye'ars ago de second husban' George kum in wid a tiny baby, sezs 'yer ez a boy baby I 'dopted. I sezs dat ez you own baby cose hits jes like yer. He denied hit, but eben now de boy ez e'zackly lak George. He's six ye'rs ole en gwine ter school. I'se got mah hands full tryin' ter raise 'im 'lone. W'en George died he had a small inshorance policy. I paid mah taxes, I owns dis home, en bought mahself three hogs. I sold two en kilt one. Den I got three mor' jes' a short time ago. Sum kind ob zeeze got among dem en dey all d'ed.

TENNESSEE NARRATIVES

Yas I'se voted four er five times, but neber had any frens in office. I don' think dis white-black mar'iage should be 'lowed. Dey should be whupped wid a bull whup.

As far as I know de ex-slaves hab wuked at diff'ent kins ob jobs en now sum I know ez in de po-house, sum git' in relief order en urthers ez lak mahself, hab dere homes en gettin' 'long bes' dey kin. I needs milk en cod liver oil fer dis lettle boy but can't buy it.

I dunno nothin' 'bout slave uprisin's. De songs I member ez:

"All Gawds Chilluns up Yonder."
"I want ter Shout Salvation."
"Down by de River Side."

INTERVIEW: NARCISSUS YOUNG
Rear 532 1st Street No.
Nashville, Tennessee

"I'se 96 y'ars ole. Bawn in slavery en mah marster wuz Isham Lamb en mah missis wuz Martha Lamb. Mah mammy d'ed w'en I wuz three y'ars ole en I wuz raised in de house 'til I wuz big 'nuff ter wuk out in de fiels wid de uthers. Mah missis l'arn me ter sew, weav en spin. I also he'lped ter cook en wuk in de house. Atter I got big'er I went ter chuch wid mah white folks en had ter set wid urther slaves in dat part ob de chuch whar nobody but slaves would be 'lowed. In slavery I'se git no money fer wuk'n but I don' steal as mah white folks sho gib me en de uther slaves plenty good things ter eat. Clothes good 'nuff fer anybody, candy, en we went ter parties en urther places, en w'at else could I'se wan'?"

"Mah missis l'arned me ter pray, "Now I lay me down ter sleep. I pray de Lawd mah soul ter keep, but if I should die 'fore I wake, I pray de Lawd mah soul ter tek." I jined de Primitive Baptist Chuch w'ile young en b'en dere ebe'y since."

"I member de ole song back dere, "Rock a Bye Baby, Yo Daddy's gon' a Huntin' ter git a Rabbit Skin ter put de Baby in."

"I wuz whup'd by mah missis fer things dat I ought'n dun, but dat wuz rite. De hahdest whup'in she eber gib me wuz 'bout two hen aigs. I had gathured de aigs in a bucket en tuk dem ter de house en I se'd de big fier in de fier-place so I tuk out two ob de aigs en put dem in de hot ashes ter bake. Mah missis se'd de aigs en axed who put dem dere. I tole her I didunt do hit, but she knowed I did. So she tole me she don' keer 'bout de two aigs, but dat she wuz gwine ter whup me fer tellin' a lie. Dey don't raise chilluns lak dat now."

"I don't b'leeve in Niggers en whites ma'rin' en I wuz raised by de "quality" en I'se b'leeves eber one should ma'rie in dere culor."

"I think de young peeples ob ter day ez dogs en sluts, en yer kin guess de rest."

"One day 'bout 12 o'clock we se'd de Yankee soldiers pas' our house. De missus hid her fine things, but dey don' kum on de place. All us Niggers run ter de cellar en hid. We found de sugah barrels en we scracht 'round fer sum sugah ter eat."

"One time de Ku Klux Klan kum ter our house but dey harm nobody. Guess day wuz lookin' fer sum slave er sum one fum 'nother plantation widout dere marster's pass."

"I se'd a lot ob sta'rs fall one time but dey neber teched de groun'. En I members seein' a comet wid a long bright shinin' tail."

"Atter freedom all de slaves lef' de plantation but I stayed dere a long time. I kum ter Nashville ovah thurty y'ars ago en I'se wuk'd as cook en house wuk'r twenty y'ars fer one party; eleben y'ars fer 'nother, en menny y'ars fer 'nother. I knows you won't b'leeve me but at one time I weigh ovuh 400 pounds, but now I'm nothin' but skin en bon'. (She weighs at least 200 pounds now). I bekum feeble en couldn't wuk out, en eber since den I'se bin kum' up a mountain, but now I git he'ps by de Social Security."

TRANSCRIBER'S NOTES

Corrected the typos per handwritten instructions. The inconsistencies in spelling and punctuation have been left as in the original text, except for adding the missing opening and closing quotation marks for consistency in certain interviews.

One word at the bottom of page 25 was illegible, but upon careful examination at high magnification, and considering that the other interviewers asked whether families were divided, my best guess is the word may be men: Nebber knowed ob any plantashuns men be divided.

TENNESSEE NARRATIVES

Historic Publishing Former Slave Narrative & Interviews Original Compilations Series™

VOLUME I: *Former Female Slave Narratives & Interviews: From Ex-Slaves in the States of Arkansas, Florida, Louisiana, Tennessee, Texas, and Virginia. With Photographs.* ISBN:978-1-64227-007-5

American slave narratives are a unique and fascinating historical resource. Although, the narratives have their contextual limitations-they are an invaluable primary source that allows one to gain insight pertaining to slaves from their own perspective.

Former Female Slave Narratives is a product of the author's interest in the institution of slavery in all its facets. The narratives and interviews contained in this volume were selected based on a specific set of variables and criteria. It is the intent of the author to present narratives that documented slave life, folklore, the Civil War, and Emancipation. In addition, the author has given special attention to include female slaves who were house slave and field workers. The various subjects were chosen in an attempt to give the readers historical and social context of slavery in America. Moreover, we have chosen to include female narratives from a variety of states.

VOLUME II: *Former Slave Narratives & Interviews: From the States of Kentucky and Georgia.* ISBN: 978-1642270112

Alabama WPA Slave Narratives: From Interviews With Former Slaves. ISBN: 978-1642270259

TENNESSEE SLAVE NARRATIVES

PREPARED FOR PUBLICATION BY
HISTORIC PUBLISHING
All Rights Reserved
San Antonio, Texas
©2017

www.ingramcontent.com/pod-product-compliance
Lightning Source LLC
Chambersburg PA
CBHW020302030426
42336CB00010B/864